indexed
2/99

D0459018

3 3029 04018 3279

SACRAMENTO PUBLIC LIBRARY
828 "I" STREET
SACRAMENTO, CA 95814

FEB - - 1999

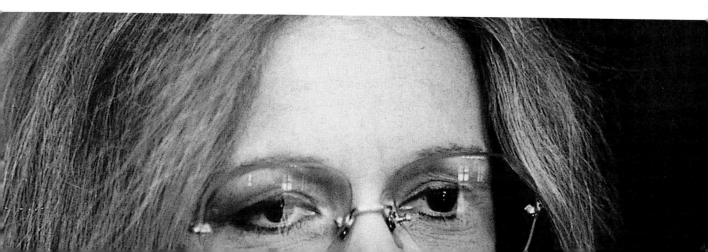

EXTRAORDINARY Jewish AMERICANS

by Philip Brooks

Children's Press®
A Division of Grolier Publishing
New York   London   Hong Kong   Sydney
Danbury, Connecticut

Library of Congress Cataloging-in-Publication Data
Brooks, Philip, 1963-
Extraordinary Jewish Americans / by Philip Brooks
p. cm. — (Extraordinary people)
Includes bibliographical references and index.
Summary: Presents short biographies of more than sixty Jewish
Americans who have flourished in careers including law, finance,
entertainment, writing, politics, and science.
ISBN 0-516-20609-5 (lib. bdg.)   0-516-26350-1 (pbk.)
1. Jews—United States—Biography—Juvenile literature. 2. United
States—Ethnic relations—Juvenile literature. [1. Jews—United
States—Biography. 2. Ethnic relations.] I. Title. II. Series.
E184.J5B7429 1998
920'.0092924073—dc21
[B]   97-37535
                                                                      CIP
                                                                      AC

©1998 Children's Press®, a Division of Grolier Publishing Co.
All rights reserved. Published simultaneously in Canada.
Printed in the United States of America.
1 2 3 4 5 6 7 8 9 10 R 07 06 05 04 03 02 01 00 99 98

Contents

54

Louis Dembitz Brandeis
1856–1941
Supreme Court
Justice

74

Stephen S. Wise
1874–1949
Influential
American Rabbi

91

**The Jews
Who Created
Hollywood**

59

Meyer Guggenheim
1828–1905
Copper King

78

Harry Houdini
1874–1926
Magician and
Escape Artist

96

Groucho Marx
1890–1977
Comedian

65

Alfred Stieglitz
1864–1946
Photographer
and Gallery Owner

83

Al Jolson
1886–1950
Singer and
Entertainer

100

Jack Benny
1894–1974
Comedian

70

Lillian Wald
1867–1940
Nurse

87

Irving Berlin
1888–1989
Popular
Composer

103

George Gershwin
1898–1937
Composer

106

Jewish Gangsters

122

Barney Ross
1909–1967
Champion Boxer
and War Hero

137

Arthur Miller
1915–
Playwright

111

Louise Nevelson
1899–1988
Sculptor

126

Benny Goodman
1909–1986
Band Leader

141

Julius *(1918–1953)*
and Ethel Rosenberg
(1915–1953)
Convicted as Spies

115

Hyman G. Rickover
1900–1986
Rear Admiral of
the U.S. Navy

130

Edwin Land
1909–1991
Inventor

146

Arnold "Red" Auerbach
1917–
Basketball Coach
and Executive

119

Jascha Heifetz
1901–1987
Violinist

134

Jonas Salk
1914–1995
Developed
Polio Vaccine

149

**Jewish Americans
and the Civil
Rights Movement**

155

Leonard Bernstein
1918–1990
Conductor and Composer

175

Maurice Sendak
1928–
Children's Author

190

Larry King
1933–
Talk Show Host

161

Betty Friedan
1921–
Women's Rights
Advocate

179

Beverly Sills
1929–
Opera Singer
and Administrator

194

Gloria Steinem
1934–
Women's Rights
Advocate

165

Henry Kissinger
1923–
Secretary of State

182

Ruth Bader Ginsberg
1933–
Supreme Court
Justice

197

Sandy Koufax
1935–
Baseball Pitcher

169

Elie Wiesel
1928–
Author

186

Dianne Feinstein
1933–
United States
Senator

202

Woody Allen
1935–
Comedian,
Filmmaker

Who *Are* the American Jews?

by Rabbi Daniel Friedman

The story of the American Jewish community is so amazing, it might sound as though someone made it up. One hundred and fifty years ago, there were barely 50,000 Jews in America. Today, with a Jewish population of 6 million, there are more Jews in America than in any other country in the world, including Israel.

Most of the Jews who immigrated to America could not speak or read English. Yet, they or their children became some of this country's most distinguished writers, scholars, and composers. Almost single-handedly, they created the Broadway musical and the motion picture industry. A large majority of American humorists and comedians are Jewish. Although Jews have never represented more than 3.5 percent of America's total population, more than one-third of America's Nobel Prize winners have been Jews. A similar percentage of the country's college professors and one-fourth of its wealthiest citizens are Jews.

Who are these people? How did they become so successful here? What explains their remarkable creativity in so many different fields?

Before we can understand the answers to these questions, a common misunderstanding about the Jews must be corrected. They are not a religious community, although many people consider the Jews, first and foremost, united by religion. The Jews, as you may know, are a very old people whose history goes back three thousand years to biblical times. Yes, the religion known as Judaism is part of that history, and for most of their past, their religion was an important bond among them. In modern times, however, many Jews—including almost all of the people you will meet in this book— have become secular, or cultural, Jews. That is, they view their "Jewishness" much as many African-Americans, Italian-Americans, and Irish-Americans see their heritage. Most American Jews feel united with other Jews not by religious beliefs, but by culture, history, and a sense of kinship. They are "related" to one another, as if they were members of a large, extended family connected by birth and common experience, rather than shared beliefs.

During the past two centuries, a dramatic change has transformed the Jewish people. They moved out of the small European villages and towns where they had been confined for centuries, and where the synagogue was the center of life. As they have moved away from this past, their religion— Judaism—became less and less significant to them. As they entered the New World and were exposed to non-religious culture and education, they left behind the ancient beliefs and practices of Judaism that had been passed down from generation to generation. Upon arriving in America, especially from the 1880s through the 1940s, the Jews found that being Jewish was no longer the disadvantage it had been for centuries. Now they were allowed opportunities never before available to them. They were able to enter occupations previously closed to them. They could move about freely and live among many other groups of people. For the first time in two thousand years, Jews enjoyed the same rights as others. In this new land, they found exciting opportunities for achievement and success. They were able to advance as far as their abilities and talents took them without being stopped by the barriers that had once blocked their way in their European homelands.

At first, they did not feel entirely "at home" in the United States. A distance still separated them from other Americans. Jewish immigrants had brought with them foreign mannerisms and foods, and ways of speaking and dressing that made them seem different from native-born Americans. Discrimination against Jews in certain professions, colleges, industries, and even neighborhoods made Jews *feel* different. This sense of "apartness" worked to their advantage. They were able to see the United States from a unique point of view. From their perspective as outsiders, they could figure out what makes the nation tick, what makes it different from other countries, what is special about its people and its spirit. They wrote articles and novels and songs that captured the essence of what the United States is all about. They seemed to understand the distinctive features of American life because they were newcomers and could stand back and see it more clearly then those more accustomed to American culture. Perhaps this perspective as outsiders explains their ability to create new music, literature, and even clothing (blue jeans, for example) that became known as distinctively American.

These newly arrived Jews and their children tended to be very ambitious. Now that there were no barriers to hold them back, they worked hard to succeed. They saw no limit to what they could create and achieve in this wondrous land of opportunity that rewarded success so handsomely. Having come from a background that placed a high value upon scholarly achievement, Jews were particularly highly motivated to excel in intellectual fields and in professions that required a high degree of education and discipline.

In addition, Jews felt they had to prove themselves before they would be fully accepted here. Perhaps they could not quite believe that at last they had found a home where they would not be persecuted, where their identity as Jews would not be held against them, and where they could compete as equals alongside people from various backgrounds and cultures. In order to satisfy themselves, as well as the world around them, that this land was different—that here they could be really "at home"—they struggled to make it their home. They helped to create its popular culture—its movies and music and entertainment media. They became first-rate scholars, doctors, lawyers, accountants, and merchants.

Gradually, the sense of being different diminished. Jews found that they were very much like other Americans—"only more so." Although they do not share the religion of most Americans (they are not Christians), their basic philosophy of life, their values, interests, and ambitions are not much different from those of other Americans. They now go to the same schools, work in the same professions, eat the same foods, and live in the same neighborhoods. Indeed, today there is concern that Jewishness is itself in danger of disappearing because first the religious beliefs and then the cultural ties that once bound Jews to one another are weakening. There is also the possibility that the remarkable creativity exhibited by the earlier generations of American Jews—when they thought of themselves as outsiders—may be subsiding, now that Jews are settled in and feel "at home" here.

You will notice that most of the people represented in this book are over the age of forty. They were born during the period when the feeling of distinctiveness was still very strong among American Jews. Since the 1950s, that feeling has all but vanished. Whether Jews will continue, in the twenty-first century, to match their accomplishments in the twentieth century is unclear. Maybe creativity and ambition are inspired partly by a sense of feeling different from others, and now that Jews have lost their feeling of distinctiveness their accomplishments will be less notable.

Whatever their future may be, it is clear that Jewish Americans have responded generously to the freedom and security they found here. Like other religious and ethnic groups that came to this country seeking safety and opportunity, the Jews have helped to create the America that all of us enjoy and cherish today.

Introduction:
Anti-Semitism and Assimilation

It is one of the most basic lessons taught in American history: George Washington, Benjamin Franklin, Thomas Jefferson, and all of the other "founding fathers" created the United States of America. And it is certainly true that these brilliant, courageous men wrote the Declaration of Independence and the Constitution, and helped fight the battles that allowed the nation to be born. But the United States they created was more of an idea than a reality. It was the endless arrival of thousands of mostly poor and oppressed men, women, and children that built the United States into a nation the founding fathers could not possibly have imagined.

Immigrants explored and settled the western regions of North America in the 1800s. Immigrants became farmers and provided labor for the Industrial Revolution. Immigrants and their offspring entered the armed forces and helped to win World War I and World War II. American immigrants found cures for diseases and put human beings on the moon for the first time, wrote popular music, and made fortunes in business. Each successive wave of Europeans, Africans, Asians, and Latinos has made the United States a stronger, richer, and more exciting place to live.

The first trickle of Jewish immigrants to North America consisted of adventurers who risked all to come to the colonies in the 1600s in hopes of finding religious freedom and prosperity. Later, during the 1850s, tens of thousands of Jews boarded ships bound for New York to escape hunger and revolution in Central Europe. An even larger wave of immigration brought three million persecuted and impoverished Jews from Eastern Europe to the United States between 1865 and 1914.

Many Jews who came to this country in the late 1800s ended up working as peddlers. Carrying a heavy pack loaded with pots and pans, needles and thread, or simple clothing, they walked west and ended up settling all over the United States. Others were skilled craftspeople who got off the boat in New York City and went immediately to work as cigar rollers, tailors, or shoemakers. During the years leading up to the Civil War, cotton became a valuable crop, and the number of Jewish planters increased in the South. And as the United States spread west, Jews bought and sold land in the new states and territories. As Jewish Americans became established citizens, they rose to the ownership ranks of banks, railroads, and shipping and insurance companies. Two Jews, Benjamin Seixas and Ephraim Hart, were among the founders of today's New York Stock Exchange in 1792.

When Adolf Hitler rose to power in Germany and began a military takeover of Europe in 1935, another wave of European Jewish immigrants entered the United States. They were soon followed by some of those who survived Nazi concentration camps. During the 1970s and 1980s, many Jews emigrated from the Soviet Union to find religious freedom. The overriding desire of all these Jewish immigrants has always been to become "good Americans."

What is most remarkable is how successful so many of these people were in their new home. Jews have never accounted for more than about 4 percent of the U.S. population. Yet, in writing and editing this book, literally hundreds of Jewish Americans had to be omitted. The history of the motion picture industry, colleges and universities, medicine, music, literature, and many other fields of endeavor would today be unrecognizable had Jews never come to the United States.

In addition to the relatively famous people whose stories are told here, there are countless Jewish Americans who do not appear simply because they led "ordinary" lives. But the contributions of these Jewish factory workers, small-business owners, lawyers, doctors, teachers, and rabbis ought not to be forgotten as we celebrate a handful of exceptional individuals. Because of their contributions to everyday life in the United States, Jewish Americans today enjoy greater acceptance, more freedom and safety, and are more influential than any Jewish community at any other time or place. As of 1997, Jews hold two of the nine seats on the United States Supreme Court and make up 10 percent of the Senate. In fact, few Americans pay much attention nowadays to whether a senator, justice, doctor, or farmer is Jewish.

Still, wherever there have been Jews, anti-Semitism has followed. The United States is no exception. Use of the word *anti-Semitism* to mean "the hatred of Jews" began in Germany in 1873. Journalist Wilhelm Marr used the term in his pamphlet, *The Victory of Judaism Over Germany.* At the time, Germany was experiencing great social and economic problems. Many Germans searched for someone or something to blame, a scapegoat. Marr and others falsely blamed German Jews and helped to begin a campaign of hatred and discrimination.

At many times in history, the Jews of various countries have been unfairly labeled as traitors, more loyal to their religion than to the state. Jews have suffered murder, rape, and torture at the hands of anti-Semites. During the 1800s, for instance, Russian and Polish soldiers routinely attacked Jewish villages, destroying property and inflicting physical harm on defenseless Jews in riots called "pogroms." Such crimes against Jewish civilians culminated in Nazi Germany's systematic killing of six million Jews between 1936 and 1945, an event now known as the Holocaust.

The first record of anti-Semitism in North America came in 1654. A boatload of Jewish refugees fleeing the Spanish Inquisition in Brazil arrived in what would become New York Harbor. They were refused entrance to New Netherland by the Dutch colony's governor, Peter Stuyvesant, who claimed Jews were greedy and would exploit and cheat Christian colonists. Stuyvesant called Jews "hateful enemies and blasphemers of the name of Christ." Eventually, Stuyvesant's superiors ordered him to allow the Jews to disembark. He did so, but denied Jews the right to own property or carry arms.

During the 1890s, politicians calling themselves "populists" blamed American farmers' economic troubles on Jews. Populists claimed that greedy Jews in business and banking were plotting to enslave American Christians as part of a master plan to take over the world. Such bogus arguments were supposedly confirmed by a ridiculous publication called *The Protocols of the Learned Elders Zion*. Even today, bigots refer to this document as "proof" that Jews seek world domination.

At the same time as some poor Americans blamed their troubles on Jews, the wealthy often did their best to keep Jews out of country clubs, hotels, and resorts. One member of a rich Protestant family argued for exclusion of Jews from upper-class society. He reportedly said, "If this is a free country, why can't we be free of the Jews?"

By the beginning of the twentieth century, industrialist Henry Ford had read the *Protocols* and become obsessed with halting "the world-Jewish conspiracy." His daily newspaper, *The Dearborn Independent,* spewed hatred of "Jew financiers," "Communist Jews," and "Jewish control." Other prominent citizens spoke against such campaigns, however. In 1921, President Woodrow Wilson and former president William Howard Taft, along with one hundred other respected leaders gathered to formally denounce anti-Semitism. Remarkably, Henry Ford eventually apologized for his attacks on Jews.

Populist fervor led to the only known lynching of a Jew in the United States. In 1915, Leo Frank, a New Yorker who moved to Atlanta to run a family factory, was arrested and accused of murder. Mary Phagan, a young employee, had been found strangled in the factory. Leo Frank and a janitor were both suspects in the case. But journalists, the Ku Klux Klan, and others seized on the idea that Frank had committed the crime. One local reporter declared that: "Our little girl . . . has been perused to a hideous death by this filthy, perverted Jew of New York." Frank was convicted, but legal experts believed the janitor had been the real culprit. Georgia's governor agreed the case warranted further examination, so he commuted Frank's sentence from death to life in prison. Hearing this, an anti-Semitic mob dragged Frank out of his jail cell and killed him. Many years later, Frank's innocence of the crime was confirmed.

Just a few years after the Frank case, during the so-called "Red Scare," a group of senators met in 1919 to discuss the danger posed by Communist spies and terrorists within the United States. Many worried that Russian Jews from New York, along with other recent immigrants, posed a serious threat to national security. A number of Jewish immigrants were arrested or deported and the press stirred up prejudice against such "strangers." Later, Father Charles Coughlin and William Pelley spread similar anti-Semitic messages through use of radio and newspapers.

Anti-Semites have blamed Jews for problems ranging from the Great Depression to World War II. But the vast majority of the American public disliked anti-Semitic ideas. Politicians, religious leaders, and newspaper editors regularly spoke against Coughlin, Pelley, and others who espoused hatred of Jews.

Following the end of World War II and the discovery of the ghastly extent of Nazi crimes, anti-Semitism waned. From 1945 through the 1960s, 1970s, and 1980s, Jews made huge strides in American society. Corporations that previously did not hire Jews now regularly promote them to positions of power. Universities that previously barred Jewish students from admission now employ many Jewish professors. Though anti-Semitic incidents still occur now and again, popular opinion has always sympathized with the victims. In 1978, when American Nazi Party members sought to march in Skokie, a heavily Jewish suburb of Chicago, millions of gentiles expressed outrage and disgust.

But as the general American public's hatred of the Jews has almost disappeared, a disturbing change occurred in relations between Jews and African-Americans. Minister Louis Farrakhan of the Nation of Islam and some other African-American leaders have recycled ancient stereotypes of Jews to explain social problems within the black community. At one point, for instance, an African-American leader in Chicago accused Jewish doctors of injecting black babies with the AIDS virus. Such attacks and Jewish counterattacks have caused tension between the two groups, which were previously strongly united during the civil rights movement. In 1991, Hasidic Jews and African-Americans clashed in the Crown Heights area of Brooklyn after a Jewish driver accidentally struck and killed an African-American child. The driver was murdered by an angry mob shouting anti-Semitic slurs.

Today, many Jewish Americans ask themselves what it means to be a Jew. Does it mean that one prays in a synagogue every week and celebrates the Sabbath? Does it simply mean that one's mother was Jewish? Or does it mean eating lox and bagels on Sunday morning? Many Jewish families have now been a part of American culture for four generations. Intermarriage between gentiles and Jews along with a decreasing emphasis on religion has left many Jews with little interest in the fact they are Jewish. Some Jewish leaders fear that Jewish ethnic identity will soon be lost as Jewish Americans are completely absorbed into the mainstream. They see such "assimilation" as the end of thousands of years of Jewish history. Others believe this is simply a new chapter.

Haym Salomon

FINANCIER OF THE AMERICAN REVOLUTION
1740–1785

The United States was founded upon the idea of religious freedom and tolerance. This is one of the first things most American schoolchildren learn about the Revolutionary War. But Jews seeking such freedom in colonial America did not necessarily receive a warm welcome. In many cases they found the same bigotry they had known in Europe. By 1776, about two thousand Jews lived in the colonies. They were seen by many gentiles as outsiders who could not be trusted. One Jewish-American patriot who helped dispel such prejudice was Haym Salomon.

Salomon was born in Lissa, Poland, in 1740. Thirty-two years later, he became the first Polish Jew to emigrate to the United States. A prominent financier in Europe, Salomon quickly built a good reputation in the colonies and earned a small fortune. His new life meant much more than mere profit, however. Salomon was inspired by the ideals of Thomas Jefferson, Benjamin Franklin, and other patriots who worked to make the United States a country free of British control. Salomon loudly declared himself a patriot whenever he had the chance.

When the British took over New York in 1776, Salomon was arrested as a rebel and sent to the infamous Provost Prison. Conditions there were dreadful. Rats scurried about. Food was scarce. Prisoners died of dysentery and other terrible diseases caused by the filth and vermin. Soon, Salomon got a lucky break. The British needed an interpreter, and he spoke several European languages. Salomon was immediately removed from the prison and attached to a British army unit.

Salomon did not forget his fellow rebels who remained in Provost Prison. Though the British kept a close eye on him, he helped a number of American and French soldiers to escape. Then, in 1778, Salomon fled the British unit he was serving. In escaping from his captors, Salomon was forced to leave his wife and infant son in New York as he made his way to Philadelphia.

Alone and penniless, Salomon wrote to the Continental Congress telling them of his patriotic efforts and begging for any job that would help the cause of revolution and put food on his table. The letter was ignored. Resourceful as always, Salomon managed to begin trading in bonds and gold, and he soon built a reputation in Philadelphia as an honest and fair dealer. As soon as he earned enough money, he brought his wife and child to his new home.

Most of the hard work and sacrifice of the revolution took place on the battlefield. Salomon's contributions to the young country's struggles were quite different but were just as essential. The government desperately needed to raise money to pay its soldiers, to buy food to feed them, and to purchase guns and ammunition to arm them. Haym Salomon, as the appointed "Broker to the Office of Finance," became entrusted with selling hides, tobacco, and other agricultural products on behalf of the U.S. government. He worked tirelessly to obtain the best prices possible and to ensure that the Continental Congress gained a reputation as trustworthy money managers.

Nearly all governments rely on loans to operate. An investor who buys a U.S. savings bond, for instance, has loaned the government a sum of money that will be repaid with interest on a specific date. Today, such investors have no doubt they will be paid. In the 1770s, however, no one knew for sure how the war would turn out. Had the rebels lost, such bonds would have become worthless pieces of paper. Salomon believed deeply in the cause and knew that without sufficient funding, the Continental Army would surely be defeated by the powerful British forces. Without regard for his or his family's future, Salomon invested thousands of dollars in these risky bonds and persuaded others to do the same. Soon, he began directly lending the Continental Congress large sums of money to help equip the army and pay its debts. He even lent money freely to unpaid members of the Continental Congress so that they could feed their families and avoid debtor's prison. Many had distrusted Salomon because he was Jewish. Grudgingly, they came to see that the "Jew broker," as he was often called, was a good and decent man who truly believed in the cause of liberty. He worked himself to the point of exhaustion to see that the war was won.

After the war, Salomon gave more of his money away to the poor and helped build a new synagogue in Philadelphia. When he died suddenly in 1785, it was revealed that his fortune was gone. It became clear just how much he had given to the cause—all his money and his health as well. For many years, Salomon's family petitioned Congress for repayment of some of the money he had loaned the republic. Each new Congress examined the matter and decided nothing would be repaid, nor would his efforts be recognized with any sort of memorial. Finally, in 1941, after many failures, a statue of Haym Salomon standing beside George Washington was erected in Chicago, Illinois.

Mordecai Manuel Noah

JOURNALIST AND POLITICIAN
1785–1851

Mordecai Noah was a showman. He loved to stand in front of a crowd and loudly proclaim his opinions on issues of the day. His sharp wit earned him many listeners. As a lawyer, playwright, and journalist, Noah became the most famous Jewish American of his time.

Mordecai Noah was born in Philadelphia and spent his early years in Charleston, South Carolina. His father served in the Continental Army and fought the British in the Revolutionary War. Noah's mother died when he was only ten years old, and he was sent to live with his maternal grandfather in Philadelphia. There he became an apprentice to a gilder and wood carver. The work was challenging but did not engage young Mordecai's curiosity. Books about politics and history were his escape. He began spending many hours at the library and thus educated himself. Noah soon took a position as a clerk in the auditor's office of the United States Treasury.

In 1812, Noah returned to Charleston. Not only did he write a play called *The Wandering Boys,* he published a series of patriotic newspaper essays calling for renewed war with Great Britain. British ships controlled the high seas and restricted U.S. trade with other nations. This led to the War of 1812. Noah's blistering editorials bore the pen name "Muley Malack."

In 1813, Noah entered politics. Secretary of State James Monroe made him the U.S. ambassador to Tunis, the first time a Jew had been appointed to so high a post in the foreign service. Monroe immediately sent Noah on a secret mission of a most delicate nature. An American ship had been captured by Algerian pirates, and the ship's crew was being held for ransom. Noah was ordered to secure the crew's release for three thousand dollars per man, and was to do so without letting it be known that the U.S. government was involved, which might have led to a rash of such kidnappings.

Noah departed from Charleston, bound for Spain. En route, his ship was captured by the British, and he was held in England for two months. Following his release, Noah traveled to Cadiz in Spain—a long and uncomfortable trip, first by sea and then by land. In Cadiz, he met a man named Richard Keene who had regular contact with Algerian pirates. Keene managed to gain the release of the Americans along with four other French-speaking men from New Orleans who claimed U.S. citizenship. Noah had no specific order to pay for the release of these other four men, but he could not imagine his country allowing them to remain hostages. So he paid for their ransom from his own pocket, assuming that he would be repaid by a grateful government.

Noah was sorely mistaken. Secretary of State James Monroe suspected Noah of wrongdoing and sent him a letter that read in part: "At the time of your appointment, as Consul at Tunis, it was not known that the Religion which you profess would form any obstacle to the exercise of your consular functions." Noah was fired on grounds that he was a Jew. Proud of his religion and seeking no gain for himself by having secured the release of the hostages, Noah was outraged. When President James Madison learned of Noah's efforts—and of Monroe's response—he offered an apology. He also saw to it that Noah was repaid. Noah wrote a book about his adventure, titled *Travels in England, France, Spain, and The Barbary States,* which was published in 1819.

As a member of the Democratic Party, Noah was appointed high sheriff of New York City in 1822. In 1829, President Andrew Jackson named him surveyor of the port of New York. Later, Noah broke with the Democratic Party. As an editor of various newspapers, Noah protested corruption within the party and helped found the Whig Party as an alternative.

The exploit for which Mr. Noah became most famous was his dream of a refuge for the world's persecuted Jews. "We will return to Zion as we went forth," he wrote in 1824. Zion was the original Jewish homeland in Israel, but until 1948 the territory was not under Jewish control. Until Israel was returned to the Jews, Noah planned to establish a temporary homeland for the displaced Jewish people. In 1825, he bought about 2,500 acres (1,012 hectares) of land on Grand Island near Buffalo, New York, and called it Ararat, in reference to Mount Ararat (the place where, according to the biblical story, Noah's ark came to rest after the flood). Mordecai Noah then appointed himself "Governor and Judge of Israel" and invited all the world's homeless Jews to join him in this new settlement. A brick-and-wood monument on the eastern side of the island carried this inscription: "Ararat, a City of Refuge for the Jews, founded by Mordecai M. Noah in the month of

Tishri 5586 [September 1825 on the Hebrew calendar] and in the Fiftieth Year of American Independence."

On a sunny September day in 1825, a huge procession traveled from Buffalo, New York, to dedicate Ararat on the Niagara River. The parade included Buffalo's most prominent citizens, a marching unit of the militia, American Indians in full ceremonial dress, and freemasons in robes. Noah himself wore crimson robes trimmed in ermine. He was cheered enthusiastically by the crowd, who enjoyed the spectacle of a royal procession in the middle of Buffalo.

Noah led the parade to the banks of the river. At this point, an unfortunate oversight nearly ruined the day. Not nearly enough boats had been hired to carry everyone across the river to Ararat. Noah himself was unable to cross. In fact, he had yet to see the property he had purchased. A nearby church was used for an impromptu dedication. Outside the church, the ceremony closed with a twenty-one-gun salute and hats tossed into the air. Despite the hoopla, not a single Jew came to Buffalo for the purpose of living in Ararat. After this failure, Noah began championing the idea of a Jewish return to Palestine. (It would be more than a century before this dream was realized.)

In 1826, Noah married Rebecca Esther Jackson, with whom he raised a family of six sons and one daughter. In 1841, New York Governor William H. Seward named Noah an associate judge on the court of sessions, an office he soon resigned in order to return to journalism. Until the end of his life, Noah wrote plays and edited various publications including *The Union, Noah's Times,* and *Weekly Messenger.* His last book, *Gleanings from a Gathered Harvest,* was an 1845 collection of his newspaper essays. Mordecai Noah died of a "stroke of apoplexy" six years later at age sixty-six.

Judah Philip Benjamin

LAWYER AND CONFEDERATE STATESMAN

1811-1884

Judah P. Benjamin was a man born at the wrong time and raised in the wrong place. He grew up in the American South during the years leading up to the Civil War. While northern states wanted to free the millions of African slaves who had been brought here as farm laborers, southern states depended on those unpaid workers to produce cheap cotton and other products. This argument would eventually contribute to all-out war between the North and South. Benjamin was a brilliant man, but even his great intellect did not allow him to see that there is no possible justification for enslaving another person.

Judah Benjamin was born in 1811 in the British West Indies. His parents soon moved to Charleston, South Carolina, and at age fourteen, he entered Yale University. All of Benjamin's professors spoke about the boy's magnificent mind but went on to say he did not make the most of his obvious talents. He never graduated from Yale. It is unclear exactly what happened, but he appears to have run wild during his time in New Haven and violated university rules. Benjamin was not terribly upset about leaving college. He moved to New Orleans, studied law, and became a lawyer at age twenty-one. Sharp-minded and argumentative, yet willing to listen to another person's reasoning, he was well suited to his new profession. Benjamin soon became famous as one of the nation's great legal minds.

In 1843, President Franklin Pierce offered Judah Benjamin a position on the United States Supreme Court. This was a great honor, but Benjamin declined it. He decided he could better serve his country—and his own ambitions—by running for state office. He became a member of the Louisiana State Legislature, and then in 1852, Benjamin won a seat in the United States Senate. As a freshman senator, he soon became embroiled in the worst crisis this country has ever known. Slavery and other issues were tearing the nation apart. The United States was gaining two new territories, Kansas and Nebraska. Would slavery be allowed there? Southerners believed they had every right to keep slaves on any land they owned. The North wanted these new territories to be free. There would be no compromise.

Benjamin was named to speak on behalf of the South. He argued brilliantly. Even those who disagreed with his position could not help but be impressed with his speaking ability. He gained a new reputation as a great orator.

As the slavery debate in Congress grew more intense, some senators engaged in personal attacks on fellow members. Benjamin was portrayed as a traitorous Jew by some northern senators. Benjamin never hid the fact he was Jewish and spoke out against those who used religious slurs against him.

Some Southerners began calling for the South to secede from (to leave) the United States and form a new country built on its own values and customs. Benjamin had no interest in breaking with the Union but, in the end, he could do nothing to stop secession. Even he came to believe there was no chance to uphold southern states' rights without going to war. The South did secede in 1861 and formed the Confederate States of America. The American Civil War soon followed.

Judah Benjamin became Confederate president Jefferson Davis's most trusted adviser, and he was appointed attorney general for the Confederacy. Today, Benjamin is often referred to as the "Brains of the Confederacy." Recognizing that the South needed help from other countries in its fight, Benjamin sought official recognition for the new government from the French and British. Despite much diplomatic maneuvering, these efforts failed.

Appointed secretary of war in 1862, Benjamin was faced with a hopeless situation. Within two or three years it became apparent that the North's forces would crush the South, given the Confederacy's inferior manufacturing capabilities and poorly equipped military. In 1863 and 1864, the South suffered one horrible defeat after another, and Southerners began using Benjamin as a scapegoat. Benjamin was accused of being a traitor. Critics called him "Judas Iscariot Benjamin," and other anti-Semitic insults. He was accused of failing to adequately supply the war effort. In truth, he had no guns or other supplies to offer. The South was bankrupt, its factories lay in ruin. Not wanting to reveal this fact to the enemy, President Davis instead made Benjamin secretary of state and appointed a new secretary of war. But the South was doomed.

After the Confederate Army surrendered in April 1865, Benjamin became a hunted criminal. He fled to Florida and escaped in a tiny boat. He traveled to the Bahamas, and then to England. Disgraced, Benjamin found himself without any way of supporting himself. At fifty-four years old, forced to leave the land he loved, his life was a shambles.

Benjamin traveled to Paris to visit his wife and daughter, whom he had not seen in five years. He was offered work in Paris as a businessman, but instead he chose to live in London. Once there, he worked hard to learn the British legal system and, thanks to his great intelligence and speaking abilities, became a prominent attorney in his adopted country. He even published several important books on British law. It is very rare for someone to become a famous lawyer in two different countries. At a banquet honoring him on the occasion of his retirement in 1882, he was hailed as "the only man who held conspicuous leadership at the bars of two countries." Benjamin soon moved to Paris to live with his wife and daughter. Upon his death, having no affiliation with any Jewish organization, he was buried in a Roman Catholic cemetery.

Benjamin's place in United States history is assured. It is unfortunate that his talents and learning were used to argue on behalf of slavery, a practice which today we recognize as unjust. Even with his genius and learning, Benjamin could not see beyond the world in which he was raised. Had he been on the side of those wanting to abolish slavery, he might today be recognized as an American hero. Instead, he is an interesting footnote to the sad history of the Civil War.

Adam Gimbel

MERCHANT
1817–1896

Many of the Jews who came to the United States before the Civil War became peddlers. They traveled from town to town carrying heavy packs on their backs. They sold simple items to people who lived far from any store: sewing needles, thimbles, scissors, spools of thread, shoelaces, and yarn. One such man, Adam Gimbel, came from Bavaria in Germany to New Orleans in 1836. He got off the boat and looked around. So here was the country where he would make his fortune! He saw a busy, dirty port city filled with businessmen, sailors, laborers, and criminals. Gimbel was twenty years old. The money in his pocket—about five dollars—represented every cent he owned, but he was not worried. Gimbel had heard, like so many others before and after him, that anyone willing to work hard could be a success in the United States.

He began working at odd jobs on the waterfront, cleaning, painting, helping to load and unload ships. He did anything to earn a few dollars. With his money, he bought merchandise to resell. Soon enough, he loaded up a heavy knapsack with sewing supplies, a few pots and pans, and anything else he thought he could sell, and started walking. Over the next seven years, he made his way to nearly every town in the Mississippi Valley.

It must have seemed achievement enough when Gimbel had earned enough money to set up a tiny store in half of a dentist's office. At least he could rest his poor feet. He chose Vincennes, Indiana, as his home base. He liked the town and believed that as Americans moved westward, the town would grow, too.

In 1842, the country faced tough economic times. More stores were closing than were opening. But Adam Gimbel still believed that if he worked hard and sold quality goods at a fair price, his business would prosper. So he accepted an offer to take over the rest of the building and expanded his store. He called it the "Palace of Trade." It looked like a plain old general store, but it was a little different from other general stores.

People living on the Western frontier believed that merchants would often cheat their customers to make a quick dollar. This was not Gimbel's policy. He gave refunds to anyone not completely satisfied with his goods, even if the customer's complaint was unfair. He hung a sign where all could see it:

If anything said or done in this store looks wrong, or is wrong,
we would have our customers take it for granted that
we shall set it right as soon as it comes to our knowledge.

Gimbel went so far as to have advertisements printed that said, "Fairness and equality to all patrons, whether they be residents of the city, plainsmen, traders or Indians." Also, he charged the same price on any purchase, whether the customer paid in cash or in trade. This policy helped many farmers and traders. It also created loyal shoppers.

Building a business based on a reputation for fairness and good value was a new idea. Gimbel went further. Traveling even a dozen miles was treacherous in those days. So Gimbel tried to carry all the merchandise a family might need. At the Palace of Trade, customers could buy lace for a new dress, a shovel, a book to read, or any of a variety of many other items. Gimbel had invented the department store.

Adam Gimbel always sought to earn a customer's long-term loyalty. His vision created an enterprise that would provide very profitable work for generations of Gimbels. He married and had seven sons, all of whom eventually entered the family business. In 1887, Gimbel and his sons opened a modern Gimbel's Department Store in Milwaukee, Wisconsin. The store was a huge success, and the Gimbels began looking for other cities in which to open their stores. Partly because Gimbel's wife's family was from Philadelphia, the next store opened there in 1894. When Adam retired the following year, his son, Isaac, took over the presidency.

Isaac and his young son Bernard dreamed of opening a glorious store in New York City. Competition in New York was fierce, but the Gimbels believed their philosophy would make their store stronger than its competitors. In 1910, Isaac and Bernard Gimbel built an eleven-story store in the center of New York's shopping district. They hired and trained a staff of five thousand people. Gimbels became the biggest and best department store in the city. Over the next seventy-five years, the Gimbel family opened stores across the country and built an immense corporation. The heavy pack on Adam Gimbel's back had grown to an enterprise worth more than $600 million!

The Gimbel Brothers Department Store in New York City in the early 1900s

Adam Gimbel's descendants still owned and operated the business into the 1990s. His revolutionary ideas on how best to build a retail business are standard practice today. But Gimbel stands as the first major retailer to make customer satisfaction his first priority.

Levi Strauss

BLUE JEANS MANUFACTURER
1829–1902

Certain products have become such a familiar part of our everyday lives that we can hardly imagine the United States—or the world—without them. Henry Ford's automobile and Coca-Cola are a couple of examples. Levi Strauss created another—blue jeans.

Like many other Jews of his era, Levi Strauss immigrated to the United States and became a peddler. He came from Germany, where his family struggled under harsh anti-Jewish restrictions. He was the youngest of six children and could see few prospects to escape poverty and oppression in his native land. So two years after his father died, Strauss came to New York City.

The year was 1847 and New York bustled with other immigrants from all over the world. All of them hoped the United States would make good on its promise of wealth and happiness for anyone willing to work hard and fit in. But in many ways, life was not much easier here than it had been in Europe. Strauss moved west to Louisville, Kentucky, and made a meager living selling thread, needles, yarn, thimbles, and combs on the frontier. He carried a 100-pound (45-kilogram) pack over the hills of Kentucky all day. Still, in the United States a Jew could earn a living and faced little persecution because of his religion. So Strauss felt lucky.

Soon, in hopes of earning a few more dollars, Strauss began peddling men's pants made from a light cotton that was imported from Genoa, Italy. People called the pants "Genovese" (jeen-oh-VEE-zee) which later was shortened to "jeans." These pants looked nothing like the blue jeans worn today. They were simply plain cotton trousers. For several years, Strauss trudged the hills selling his jeans to farmers.

Then, in 1853, Strauss was lured West by the gold rush. Men from all across the United States flocked to San Francisco hoping to get rich digging and panning for gold in California's mountains and streams. Strauss and his brother-in-law David Stern caught the fever, too. They boarded a ship bound for San Francisco but they did not plan to prospect for gold. Instead, they carried bolts of cloth they hoped to sell to others who were struck with gold fever. Strauss and Stern ended up selling much of the cloth on the way there. In fact, all Strauss had left was some canvas he had planned to sell to tent makers. But when a miner wanted to buy a pair of pants, Strauss sent this canvas fabric to a tailor to fill the order. The miner liked Strauss's heavy-duty canvas trousers. Soon, other miners came to Strauss wanting a pair of the sturdy pants.

At first, Strauss sold his pants by climbing through California's harsh terrain to visit miners in their camps. But demand was so great that he was soon able to hire a salesman to do this part of the work for him. He established a store called "Levi Strauss and Company" and business grew steadily. By 1866, Strauss, two of his brothers, and a pair of brothers-in-law ran Levi Strauss and Company's manufacturing operation. They had a four-story building in San Francisco and an eastern office in New York City.

In 1873, Strauss signed a partnership agreement with a Nevada tailor named Jacob W. Davis. Davis made a few changes in Strauss's pants. He had noticed that pockets tended to tear because miners filled them with heavy ore. So he reinforced the pockets with metal rivets at the seams. Further, Davis decided to stitch Straus's pants with orange thread to match the color of the rivets. To make the jeans even more distinctive, he stitched a V-shaped design on the back pocket. And right onto the seat of the pants he stitched a tag that read "a new pair FREE." The tag guaranteed a new pair of jeans to anyone whose pants ripped.

Strauss ran an ad for the new and improved jeans: "Excellently adapted to use of those engaged in manual labor." His pants were made for "miners, lumberjacks, cowboys, and teamsters." He called this new version of his product "lot #501." Davis's ideas and Strauss's ad campaign led to a boom in business. Today it is hard to imagine what United States fashion would be like without Levi Strauss's lot #501. In 1876, Strauss sold $200,000 worth of lot #501 and thus had completed his rise from poor immigrant to struggling peddler to successful businessman. He had become rich.

Levi Strauss now stood as a testament to the truth of the dream that had lured him across the Atlantic Ocean. Still, he worked tirelessly. Friends urged him to relax and enjoy his success. He told them that since he had no wife and family his business was his life.

In 1886, Strauss decided to pursue other business interests. He served on many corporate boards and owned dry goods, transportation, and communication companies. Having no children of his own, he turned operation of

Today, millions of people wear Levi's jeans, which were invented for use by miners more than a century ago by Levi Strauss.

the pants business over to his younger sister's sons. In his later years, Strauss became a philanthropist. He built homes for the aged and orphanages for Jewish, Roman Catholic, and Protestant children. He also set up a number of scholarship funds to help poor children attend college.

When Levi Strauss died, he left his business and $5 million to his younger sister and her sons. An additional $1.6 million in gold was divided among various charities, friends, and relatives. Strauss was, by all accounts, a very kind man who said little about himself. Strauss seems, ultimately, to have been a lonely man. His newfound wealth did not ease his sadness. In a rare interview for the San Francisco *Bulletin,* he said, "I don't think money brings friends to its owners. In fact, often the result is quite the contrary."

Uriah P. Levy

NAVY COMMODORE
1792–1862

Uriah P. Levy could not bear to watch. A United States Navy sailor who had violated a minor rule had been stripped of his shirt and tied to the ship's mast. The sailor was about to be punished for a rules infraction by being flogged with a heavy leather whip. When the whip slashed the sailor's back, Levy turned away in horror. He vowed that he would do all in his power to abolish the barbaric practice. This was not what he had expected of the United States Navy.

When Levy was fourteen years old, he had left Philadelphia to fulfill his dreams of exploring the high seas. He became an apprentice on a merchant ship. In 1812, still only twenty years old, Levy was named an officer on a ship called the *Argus,* which set sail to deliver goods to France. During this time, the British had set up a naval blockade around France as part of their long fight with Napoleon. The *Argus* ran through Britain's blockade and delivered its goods to France with little trouble. On its way back, however, the *Argus* was intercepted by a heavily armed British frigate. Levy and his fellow sailors knew they were in deep trouble. Outgunned, they fought until the *Argus* sank, full of holes. Levy was rescued and thrown in a British prison for sixteen months.

The battle left a deep impression on him. He had realized that some of the *Argus's* bravest sailors were African-Americans, Jamaicans, and others of low social rank. The navy often looked down on such men and ignored them when granting promotions.

Levy's own suffering, however, was only beginning. He had made several powerful enemies. A few naval officers disliked him simply because he was Jewish. They felt he did not "know his place." In 1817 when he was promoted to the rank of lieutenant, these officers protested. Ultimately, their protests were ignored by their more open-minded superiors. For his part, Levy defended his name and religious faith against all attacks. Once, he was even challenged to a duel. He shot and fatally wounded his challenger.

In 1839, when Levy was named commodore of the U.S.S. *Vandalia,* he made sure that promotion on his ship was based purely on seamanship, regardless of race, religion, or social class. This angered many in the navy establishment who believed only so-called "gentlemen" should be made officers.

After the war, Levy further annoyed those who wanted the navy to remain just as it was. He launched a campaign to outlaw flogging as a means of punishment. Despite resistance from his highest superiors, Levy would not be silenced. Soon, the navy had to admit that the practice was inhumane and served only to damage morale. Flogging became a thing of the past. Levy considered the new rule outlawing the brutal practice to be the greatest achievement of his life because he had lessened the suffering of countless men. Levy's enemies within the navy caused him to be court-martialed six different times for allegedly ignoring various regulations. In each case, Levy was cleared of all charges. In 1855, his detractors succeeded in calling a congressional board of inquiry to examine his entire naval career. These officers believed that at long last, Levy would be booted out of the service. But far from condemning any of his actions, the board's findings led to another promotion. Levy was praised for his forward-looking ideas, and he was named commodore of the navy's entire Mediterranean fleet. Thousands of men and dozens of ships were now under his steady and just command.

While the navy took up much of Uriah Levy's time, he had other interests. Thomas Jefferson was one of his heroes. When Levy learned that Monticello, Jefferson's Virginia home, had fallen into disrepair, he bought it. He invested a great deal of his time and money to ensure that the magnificent house and gardens were restored and preserved for future generations. Jewish affairs also were important to him. In addition to charitable work on behalf of Jewish organizations, he helped found the first synagogue in Washington, D.C., and served as its first president.

The navy has paid tribute to Levy in several ways. During World War II, a destroyer was named the U.S.S. *Levy*. A few years later, the armed forces built its first Jewish chapel on the grounds of the huge naval base at Norfolk, Virginia. Today, the Commodore Uriah P. Levy Jewish Chapel celebrates his life and legacy.

Emma Lazarus

POET

1849–1887

Emma Lazarus was widely known as the "poet of the oppressed." She earned the distinction despite suffering little oppression directly. For the most part, Lazarus led a comfortable life. She grew up in New York City with plenty of money, the daughter of kind, educated parents who were deeply devoted to her. But Lazarus chose to step outside her safe and pleasant world. She empathized with immigrants living in poverty, and devoted herself to helping them in any way she could. Most of all, she called attention to their plight through her poetry.

As a girl, Lazarus was sickly and shy. Believed by her parents to be too frail to attend school outside the house, she was educated by private tutors. She became a devoted reader and especially loved classical Greek literature and novels by British and American authors. But poetry became the center of Emma's life. She kept a journal in which she wrote down her thoughts, but when whe was young, she was too shy to share them with anyone.

Lazarus soon got over such "stage fright." In 1867, while still a teenager, she published her first book, *Poems and Translations.* The book did not go unnoticed. The great American poet Ralph Waldo Emerson was deeply impressed by Lazarus's work. He wrote a letter inviting her to spend a week with him in Concord, Massachusetts. The two became instant friends and exchanged letters for the rest of Emerson's life.

Throughout these years, Lazarus was devoted to her family, learning, literature, and her writing. She considered herself Jewish, but this was not an important part of her life. She once said that she never much liked "Jewish things." Then, two things happened. First, she read a book by a woman named George Eliot called *Daniel Deronda.* The novel argued for a Jewish "revival"—a return to the strong traditions that had helped sustain so many generations of Jews. The book made a deep impression on Lazarus. At the same time, the newspapers carried stories of the Russian pogroms of 1881 and 1882. Pogroms were organized riots in which Russian soldiers attacked defenseless Jewish villagers. Jews were forced to flee their homes and businesses. Many were beaten or killed. To escape such persecution, thousands of Jewish refugees began making their way to the United States. Lazurus was surprised at how strongly she felt their suffering. She felt as if her own relatives were involved.

So Lazarus's life and work steered in a new direction. She volunteered to work with immigrants arriving at Ward's Island, near New York City. Her notebooks were soon filled with the stories and faces of the countless tired, sad, angry, and proud refugees she met there. "I am all Israel's now," she wrote one day. "Till this cloud passes I have no thought, no passion, no desire, save for my own people." The poetry Lazarus wrote became a voice for the immigrants she met each day, and for all the Jews still living under Russian rule. In print and in public meetings, she argued that the United States had a moral obligation to stand always as a beacon of hope for all people living without freedom.

Despite her good work, Emma Lazarus might today be forgotten were it not for the French government. In 1885, the United States received the Statue of Liberty as a gift from France. It took the French two years to build the statue and ship it to New York. In the meantime, efforts were started to raise money for the huge pedestal upon which the statue would stand in New York Harbor.

Mrs. Constance Harrison had the idea to raise funds through a book of poetry and sketches by famous American writers. Harrison planned to include work by Mark Twain, Walt Whitman, and many others. When Emma Lazarus was asked to contribute a poem, she immediately declared she could not write poems on demand. Such a task was against her artistic nature. But when she began to think of what the statue meant, she accepted the assignment. Two days later, the result was a sonnet titled "The New Colossus." (The title refers to The Colossus of Rhodes, a 105-foot tall statue of Helios, the Greek god of the sun. It stood on the island of Rhodes, overlooking the harbor, and was one of the Seven Wonders of the Ancient World.)

The New Colossus

Not like the brazen giant of Greek fame,
With conquering limbs astride from land to land,
Here at our sea-washed, sunset gates shall stand
A mighty woman with a torch, whose flame

Is the imprisoned lightning, and her name
Mother of Exiles. From her beacon-hand
Glows world-wide welcome; her mild eyes command
The air-bridged harbor that twin cities frame.

"Keep, ancient lands, your storied pomp!"
Cries she,
With silent lips.
"Give me your tired, your poor,
Your huddled masses yearning to breathe free,
The wretched refuse of your teeming shore,
Send these, the homeless, tempest-tost to me:
I lift my lamp beside the golden door!"

Lazarus's poem was inscribed on the Statue of Liberty's base and became one of the most famous pieces of American literature. Many people believe that the lines *Give me your tired, your poor/Your huddled masses yearning to breathe free* are the very essence of the melting pot that is the United States. To the millions of immigrants who came to America near the turn of the century, the poem and the statue lit the way to their new world.

Emma Lazarus believed Jewish immigration to the United States was only a temporary solution to a global problem. The persecuted Jews of Europe needed a safe haven, and she hoped to see the state of Israel established in Palestine. Lazarus became ill, however, and died of cancer in 1887 at age thirty-eight, long before Israel was born. "The New Colossus" speaks of the United States at its best and most generous and Lazarus's own story is an inspiration for people unwilling to ignore the less fortunate.

Ellis Island

During the 1600s, the Mohegan Indians called it Gull Island. It was a tiny piece of land that nearly disappeared during high tide. In 1628, when Dutch settlers discovered rich oyster beds there, they renamed it Oyster Island. In 1890, U.S. government officials decided the island would become the first immigration station in the United States. Congress passed a law creating the Bureau of Immigration and a set of rules governing admittance to the country. "Undesirables" were kept out. This group included the mentally or physically disabled; persons unable to support themselves; those convicted of crimes involving "moral turpitude" (crimes that are vile or immoral); anyone married to more than one person; and anyone carrying a "loathsome or contagious" disease.

In 1900, following a fire that destroyed most of the buildings on the island, a new red-brick and limestone station was opened. On December 17, its opening day, 2,251 immigrants were processed there. And the flow only increased. In 1906, a total of 1,100,735 immigrants arrived in the United States. The following year brought 1,004,756 more. Most of these millions of people passed through Ellis Island.

It is difficult to imagine the hardships many of them endured. First, they needed money to make the trip across the Atlantic Ocean. The passage cost some people their entire life savings. Russian and European immigrants spent between ten and twenty-two days at sea, and only a handful could afford the price of a first- or second-class cabin in which they could sleep in a private bed. Most traveled in "steerage," the way cattle were transported. In steerage, crowded together by the hundreds, men, women, and children slept in low-ceilinged rooms below deck. No portholes allowed fresh air to enter the cramped quarters, and the toilets were inadequate for so many people. It was nearly impossible to wash. To make the foul-smelling, unsanitary conditions even worse, many immigrants believed that eating fresh garlic prevented seasickness, so the smell of bad breath prevailed. During storms, immigrants were locked into these quarters so they would not be blown overboard. Lice-infested bedding, terrible food, and short rations made the trip almost unbearable. One can imagine the joy and relief such travelers must have felt when at last their ship sailed past the Statue of Liberty into New York Harbor. But the long trip to America was not yet over.

Ellis Island was the processing area for the U.S. Immigration and Naturalization Department. Potential immigrants were checked for disease and other problems before being admitted into the country. The U.S. government did not want to admit sick people who would be unable to support themselves, or who might infect citizens with contagious diseases. One can only imagine the terrible fear immigrants experienced as they and their loved ones awaited the doctors' decision. To be denied admittance meant a return trip to their country of origin and an end to their dreams of freedom.

First, immigrants were lined up in front of the main doors, divided into groups of thirty, and tagged for easier identification. From there, each group of thirty proceeded upstairs for processing. Unbeknownst to them, a doctor observed their progress up the stairway and noted anyone who experienced difficulty making the climb. At the top of the stairs lay the vast and crowded Registry Room.

The Great Hall, as it was called, rose more than 50 feet (15 meters). A maze of metal railings guided immigrants into a long slow-moving line that snaked on and on toward uniformed officials. By 1911, the railings were replaced with benches so that the exhausted immigrants could at least sit while waiting to learn their fate.

Doctors asked each immigrant to walk ahead steadily. Children as young as two were asked to do the same to prove they were healthy. An uneven gait could mean physical or mental illness—and rejection. Children's heads were examined for lice. Doctors used a special instrument to look beneath each immigrant's eyelids for signs of trachoma, a contagious eye disease that leads to blindness.

If the doctor discovered any condition requiring treatment, or in some cases deportation, he marked the immigrant's coat with chalk. Different letters indicated different conditions. An "E" meant "eyes" and almost certain rejection. Other letters stood for "hernia" or "heart" or "mental abnormality." To be marked with a strange letter sent many immigrants into a panic. But the vast majority passed the inspection with no trouble. Others were sent to a separate area for a more thorough medical examination.

Having passed inspection, immigrants moved to the back of the Registry Room. Beneath a huge American flag stood the inspector who would finally grant or withhold permission for each of them to enter the United States. One by one, each immigrant's name was called by the inspector. Many answered to a new name for the first time when called to the inspector's desk. Names considered difficult to pronounce were often altered when they boarded ship in their home countries. Others had their names "Americanized" at Ellis Island. For instance, "Katznelson" was changed to either "Katz" or "Nelson," and "Adamczak" was changed to "Adams."

Through interpreters, the inspector asked each applicant twenty-nine questions, such as whether they could read, and whether relatives awaited them in the United States. An answer that did not match the individual's paperwork could lead to detainment until the problem was corrected. Again, most people passed inspection without incident. From there, immigrants changed their European money into U.S. dollars and awaited a ferry into New York City.

This process was repeated thousands of times a day. Officials often worked twelve-hour shifts as ships lined up in the harbor filled with people hoping to build a new life.

Those who were detained pending further medical examination or paperwork problems were housed in vast dormitories. Conditions here were a great improvement over the ships. Though the dorms were hot in summer and cold in winter, food was plentiful and conditions were clean. In the dining rooms, many immigrants got their first taste of such American staples as white bread and tapioca pudding. When faced with the exotic banana, many immigrants had to be told to peel it before eating.

Time spent in detention was nerve-wracking, and impatient officials could be unsympathetic. Ellis Island's director once declared in frustration: "Aliens have no inherent right to land on American soil!"

When World War I broke out in 1914, fewer immigrant ships set sail. In 1915, only 178,416 immigrants were processed at Ellis Island. Following the Communist revolution in Russia, many Americans worried that Communists living in the United States might attempt a similar takeover. The so-called "Red Scare" of 1919 led to the deportation of people suspected of somehow conspiring to bring a Communist system to the United States. These people were detained at Ellis Island before being shipped to other countries.

During the 1920s, various restrictions slowed the number of immigrants. By 1954, declining immigration and the creation of many other stations led to the closing of Ellis Island. Through the years, many proposals were made to take over the island, tear down the buildings, and create a hospital, a gambling casino, a bible college, or a luxury hotel. But in 1965, President Lyndon Johnson ensured that the historic landmark would not be destroyed when he signed legislation making it part of the Statue of Liberty National Monument. Due to cuts in the federal budget, however, no money was spent to protect and preserve the Great Hall and other buildings on the island. They fell into disrepair.

In 1974, the Restore Ellis Island Committee was formed, and two years later President Gerald Ford approved a million-dollar restoration project. Ellis Island was remodeled into a marvelous museum dedicated to the journey made by so many. Most citizens of the United States are descendants of people who passed through the Registry Room of the Great Hall. The museum houses a library, two movie theaters, an oral-history studio, and a restaurant. In years past, millions of new Americans took a boat ride from Ellis Island to Manhattan to enter the United States for the first time; today, millions of tourists board ferries on Manhattan and ride to Ellis Island to visit the past.

The Jews and the millions of others who stood in line and waited to enter the United States between 1900 and 1950 are as much a part of the nation's history as George Washington and Thomas Jefferson. These individuals brought the new ideas and stamina that fed a growing economy and population. Today, Asians and Latinos make up the bulk of new immigrants to the United States. Such diversity continues to make the country a vibrant and changing place filled with new ideas and ambition.

Samuel Gompers

UNION ACTIVIST
1850–1924

During the mid-1800s, children in England were often expected to earn wages. Generally, only children of the well-to-do enjoyed the luxury of an education. Samuel Gompers' parents were not wealthy. When Gompers reached the age of ten, he left school and went to work as an apprentice to a local shoemaker. He earned a salary of six cents a week. Fed up with such low wages, Gompers soon gave up the idea of becoming a cobbler and took a factory job making cigars. This move increased his weekly earnings to twelve cents, but Gompers' new job did not last long. England had too many skilled cigar makers, and young Samuel Gompers soon found himself unemployed. This was not an uncommon story. A union called the Cigarmakers' Society arranged to send Samuel and his family to the United States, where cigar-rolling skills were in greater demand. Such emigration was often used as a means of decreasing unemployment in Great Britain.

In 1863, the Gompers family arrived in New York. Like so many before and after them, they were hopeful that their days of poverty would soon be over. The Gompers were only one of tens of thousands of immigrant families who arrived in the United States around this time. Many lived in terrible poverty in New York City's tenements and worked in unclean, unsafe factories. Few laws protected workers from greedy bosses. No limits had been set on the weekly hours management could demand of their employees. Many people worked ten or twelve or more hours a day, six days a week, for small wages. Even children were subjected to such labor practices.

Many devout Jews were especially upset about working on Saturdays, the traditional Sabbath. These religious families lived by sacred Jewish laws. One such law prohibited them to do any work on the Sabbath. But they had no choice. Their gentile bosses had no intention of shutting down production every Saturday. Often, Jewish immigrants wept all Saturday as they sewed garments or rolled cigars for pennies.

Samuel and his father made cigars at home for a time. The family's tiny apartment was dark and always smelled of tobacco. When he was sixteen, Samuel got a job at a cigar factory. But even with Samuel's steady wage, the Gompers family never had enough money. They felt in constant danger of falling into even worse poverty, and of being put out on the street by their landlord.

As the years wore on, Gompers grew increasingly disgusted with the way he and his fellow workers were forced to live. It was unfair that a few owners and bosses should enjoy incredible wealth while their workers had nothing. Gompers knew that workers had little power to fight unfair pay and conditions. Until their voices were joined together and raised as one, they would never be heard.

Determined to help change the system, Gompers joined a workers' union, Local 144. Unions are organizations made up of workers in the same industry who agree to act together to improve working conditions. In 1874, Gompers was elected president of Local 144. Three years later, with the help of fellow union leaders Adolph Strasser and Ferdinand Laurell, he led a strike to protest unsanitary conditions in cigar factories. Gompers and his fellow workers put down their tools, walked off their jobs, and refused to return to work until the company's owners and managers agreed to make improvements.

For a time, the company bosses did nothing. They waited for the workers to grow scared of losing their jobs and return to work. But Gompers and his fellow organizers saw to it that the union members remained united and strong. Management was forced to clean up the factories.

This small victory made Gompers hungry for more. He now understood that if labor unions could gain more power, they could change the world for the better. In 1881, Gompers attended his first national union meeting in Pittsburgh. At age thirty-one, he found himself elected vice president of the Federation of Organized Trades and Labor Unions. Five years later, he formed a group he called the American Federation of Labor (AFL). As president of the AFL, Gompers was a national spokesman for working people. His first great project was to force industry to give workers an eight-hour workday. When business leaders refused to listen to such demands, he lobbied Congress. As more and more union members began voting in national elections, congressmen grew more willing to listen to their concerns. In 1938, a law passed by Congress created the forty-hour workweek and brought the concept of workers' rights to everyone's attention.

Unions became more visible than ever during World War I (1914–18). Workers in nearly every industry helped the United States win the war by making the guns, ammunition, clothing, and food that supplied the military. Gompers was appointed by President Woodrow Wilson to the Commission for International Labor Legislation, which sought to help workers worldwide. This organization, along with ever-improving production techniques, helped workers gain a level of dignity and respect they had never known.

When Samuel Gompers died in 1924, the American Federation of Labor boasted a membership of more than five million. In 1933, President Franklin D. Roosevelt, a strong supporter of workers' rights, dedicated a statue of Gompers in Washington, D.C.

In 1950, on what would have been his 100th birthday, the U.S. Postal Service issued a stamp celebrating his contributions; Gompers was one of the first Jewish Americans so honored. And today, more than seventy years after his death, Samuel Gompers is remembered and revered by the world's workers.

Louis Dembitz Brandeis

SUPREME COURT JUSTICE
1856–1941

Early in his working life, lawyer Louis D. Brandeis became known as "Counsel for the People." He argued worthy cases without charging a fee and won nearly every one. Later, as a Supreme Court justice, Brandeis became a powerful man in Washington, D.C. In fighting relentlessly for what he believed was right and fair, Brandeis often came up against other powerful people who tried to slow or stop social progress. Such challenges failed to deter him. He truly believed that as a lawyer, judge, and social activist, it was his duty to move his country always forward, toward justice and equality.

As he was growing up, Louis came to deeply admire his uncle, Lewis Dembitz, a scholarly man interested in civil rights and other social causes. Long talks with his uncle sparked Louis's interest in the law and provided him with a sense of fairness that would guide him throughout his adult life. Louis even changed his middle name to Dembitz as a tribute to his uncle.

Throughout his youth, Louis was a brilliant student. Every school he attended showered him with awards. Such a brilliant and driven young man might have pursued any line of work he liked. But only the law appealed to Louis. His record at Harvard Law School remains the best ever achieved by any student in the history of the institution. After graduation, he quickly developed a large and profitable law practice in Boston and then New York. But such a practice did not provide Brandeis with satisfaction. Being hired to pursue another person's interests did not suit him. He disliked the idea that he was always "someone's lawyer." He would have preferred to speak on his own behalf about the things in which he believed.

During this frustrating period in his life, Brandeis met the love of his life. Alice Goldmark, his second cousin, had a sharp mind and a strong will. The two found they agreed on everything from frugal living to helping the oppressed. In fact, Alice pushed Brandeis to help lead the charge in various social causes. Together they had two daughters, to whom they were deeply devoted. Louis Brandeis loved to ride horseback and walk in the woods with his family. Until the end of his life, he worked hard but also enjoyed spending time with his family and his many friends. One of his friends was the legendary Justice Oliver Wendell Holmes, Jr., of the United States Supreme Court.

Slowly, Brandeis became known as a crusader for social justice. He was outraged to learn that many Massachusetts city and state politicians were corrupt. Elected officials regularly took bribes, or made decisions based on what might help their friends rather than the common good. Such practices represented a serious violation of the public's trust. With other prominent citizens, Brandeis formed a group called the Good Government Association. The organization ensured that voters were well informed concerning any crooked dealings by politicians running for reelection. "The politician can stand any amount of attack, but he cannot stand the opposition of the public," declared Brandeis.

Brandeis also closely examined the insurance industry and declared that fraud was rampant. Basically, not enough of the money paid into insurance companies as premiums by working men and women was ever paid out in claims. The companies made unfair profits at the expense of policy holders. Brandeis called this a "scam" and spent many years breaking the grip of insurance companies by backing legislation and persuading industry leaders to listen to their conscience. Millions of policy holders were helped by these efforts. At the end of his life, Brandeis considered such reforms to be among his greatest achievements.

Throughout his long career in the law, Brandeis distrusted big business. In the early 1900s, so-called "monopolies" loomed as a dangerous trend in the United States. Industries such as oil, steel, and railroads were dominated by a few huge corporations that fixed prices and conspired to squeeze out all competition. Brandeis, and many others, saw this as unfair to "the little guy," and he angered many powerful business leaders when he denounced such practices and fought them in the courts.

Again and again, Brandeis became involved in major labor disputes, or in battles involving the interests of the rich and powerful versus those of vulnerable common citizens. He hated exploitation and could not sit still while it went on. This made him the subject of vicious, often anti-Semitic, attacks. Brandeis had never been a religious man, nor did he know much about Jewish history. But becoming the target of such hatred inspired him to find out more about his heritage. Learning of the Jews' long history of persecution in various countries at many times prompted him to become an outspoken supporter of a Jewish homeland in Palestine.

On January 28, 1916, President Woodrow Wilson nominated Brandeis to sit on the Supreme Court. He was the first Jew accorded this honor. At first, many opposed his appointment. He had created powerful enemies over the years. Some believed no Jew should be allowed to sit on the Supreme Court. Brandeis overcame all such objections and eventually served as a Supreme Court justice for twenty-three years.

There are nine justices on the Supreme Court. Each justice votes on a given case argued before them. Few decisions are unanimous. Time and time again, Brandeis found himself in the dissenting minority along with his good friend Oliver Wendell Holmes. In fact, "Holmes and Brandeis dissenting" became a famous legal phrase. The two men did not care for the rich and powerful. They passionately pursued justice in its purest form. Many of their opinions, although in the court's minority at the time, later became law.

For each case heard before the Supreme Court, a majority and minority opinion are written and placed in the public record. Brandeis became known for writing long, exhaustive briefs (official legal documents) to back up his decisions. Holmes, already seventy-five years old when Brandeis joined the Court, dreaded reading such lengthy documents and teased Brandeis about his long-windedness. But Brandeis used writing as a tool to find out exactly what he thought about things. He did not believe in using some overall theory to view the world and making decisions based on such general rules. "I have no general philosophy," he told a reporter. "All my life I have thought only with the facts that came before me."

During the Great Depression, Brandeis sought to slow new laws that were meant to help put the economy back on its feet. Any hope for people who had lost their jobs due to the terrible economic collapse rested on such a revitalization. President Franklin D. Roosevelt, one of Brandeis's great admirers, became angry when Brandeis rejected his sweeping changes in the social welfare system. Roosevelt denounced the Court as "the nine old men." But Brandeis stood by his belief that Roosevelt's intended laws would not benefit the country.

Soon after his skirmish with the president, Justice Brandeis defended a worker who did not want to join a union. This was seen as a betrayal of organized labor, a movement he had helped push ahead. "I have defended the working people when they needed it against the tyranny of industry," he replied. "I do not propose now to see anyone subjected to a tyranny of labor."

Brandeis died in 1941 at the age of eighty-five. Seven years later, Brandeis University was established in his honor in Waltham, Massachusetts. It is one of the finest institutions of higher learning in the United States and stands as the first university to be established and sponsored by Jews.

Louis Brandeis helped to reshape the American idea of fair play. He championed the rights of the "little guy" over the greed of the "big guy" every day of his long career. Tireless in his pursuit of social justice, Louis D. Brandeis is remembered throughout the world as a truly righteous man.

Meyer Guggenheim

COPPER KING
1828–1905

During the early twentieth century, the U.S. economy was dominated by a handful of ambitious entrepeneurs. Laws preventing so-called "monopolies" had yet to be passed. This lack of government regulation made it possible for a massive corporation to control an entire industry and eliminate any smaller competitor that threatened to cut into its profits. Scottish immigrant Andrew Carnegie controlled a huge share of the country's steel production, and oil baron John D. Rockefeller made himself the richest man in the United States. Another industry giant was Meyer Guggenheim, who went from being a poor peddler to controlling much of the world's copper and other minerals.

Meyer Guggenheim and his father, Simon, came to the United States from Switzerland in 1848. Like so many of the Jews who emigrated to the United States, they hoped to escape bigotry and poverty at home. The Guggenheims were not particularly religious Jews, but they were persecuted with as much hatred as the most devout Orthodox Jews.

When the Guggenheims arrived in Philadelphia, they became peddlers. Hiking the Pennsylvanian countryside selling needles, thread, ribbons, shoelaces, and cleaning supplies out of their heavy packs was tiring, but Meyer was glad to be working for himself instead of having a boss. It was only a matter of time, he believed, until he could set down his pack and run a real business. Where Meyer Guggenheim differed from most of his fellow peddlers was that he always reinvested any profits he and his father earned into other small-business ventures. During the Civil War, for instance, he set up a company that roasted, ground, and brewed coffee with chicory flavoring. He bottled his drink and sold it to the Union Army, where it was quite popular with soldiers. The Guggenheims used the profits from their coffee sales to buy spices from the West Indies, which they then sold in America.

Then one day Meyer Guggenheim was talking with a farmer's wife who was making soap, and Meyer began hatching an idea that would allow him and his father to set down their packs for good. Most rural people made their own soap with animal fat and lye. The woman explained to Meyer that lye was relatively expensive and made more so by the fact that one company, the Pennsylvania Salt Company, controlled nearly all the state's production of the chemical. Guggenheim did some research and learned of an English chemical that served the same function as lye—but cost much less. He quickly bought huge quantities of the lye substitute and raked in huge profits by selling it to just about everyone who made soap. Soon, the Pennsylvania Salt Company was forced to buy Guggenheim's newest business—at a steep price.

By now, Guggenheim was a wealthy man with a wife and two sons who were assured of a comfortable life. But wealth and security were not what drove him. He was fascinated by business. He saw it as a game won by those who were alert, intelligent, and decisive.

Such decisiveness, and a willingness to accept risk as a part of doing business, would soon vault the Guggenheims into American history. One day an acquaintance named Charles Graham came to Guggenheim's office asking for a loan. Graham explained that he had sunk his last two thousand dollars into a Colorado silver mine and needed more money to make the investment pay off. Unrolling a crude map on Guggenheim's desk, Graham could not contain his enthusiasm as he described the mine's potential bonanza. Aware that Graham was a cautious man, and not easily excited, Guggenheim decided the opportunity was a genuinely good one. So, instead of simply loaning Graham the money, Guggenheim became a full partner in the enterprise. The two men shook hands, and the deal was done.

The new partners traveled several days by stagecoach and train to Leadville, Colorado, where the mine was located. When they finally arrived, Guggenheim stared down into a deep hole filled with black water. His confidence wavered, but the manager of the project assured him that if he had the equipment to pump out the water they would find a huge deposit of silver. Guggenheim put up another thousand dollars for pumps and returned to Philadelphia, where he found a telegram asking for yet another thousand dollars for more equipment. Again, Guggenheim complied. When further telegrams asked for more money, he reluctantly paid up again. Then, as weeks passed with no word from Colorado, he grew resigned to the fact that he had poured thousands of dollars into a watery hole in the ground, and turned his attention back to his spice business. But one day a messenger arrived with another telegram from Colorado. Disgusted, Guggenheim prepared himself to read another request for more of his hard-earned money. But the telegram read: "Rich strike—mine yielding fifteen ounces silver, sixty percent lead..." It took Guggenheim only a moment with pencil and paper to realize he was now a millionaire. He decided from that day forward to focus all his efforts on the mining business.

He sold his other businesses to finance the purchase of smelters, huge plants where metals are processed and purified, and brought his sons together in the new business. M. Guggenheim and Sons soon bought mines and built smelters all over the world. The corporation's various mineral companies dug Chilean nitrate, Mexican silver, and African diamonds. In a span of a few years, M. Guggenheim and Sons produced more than one-third of the world's copper. Guggenheim had become one of the great tycoons of the American Industrial Revolution.

Though Meyer and his sons were tough-minded businessmen, they had some sense of fair play concerning the miners who worked for them. While most workers were routinely forced to work long hours for pitifully low wages, Guggenheim's miners were relatively well treated. When a group of businessmen who owned smelters and mines got together to form a trust that would fix wages and force miners to accept whatever terms they offered, Guggenheim declined to participate. His miners worked a standard eight-hour day.

This was not the only battle Guggenheim would fight with the newly formed Smelter's Trust. When the trust ordered a complete shutdown in Colorado in hopes of raising gold and silver prices nationally, Guggenheim kept his operations open and did not raise his prices. Soon, losing millions of dollars a day because of the shutdown, the trust broke down. As a result, many of the companies were forced to sell their operations to Guggenheim

The Guggenheim Museum in New York City

at greatly reduced values. This was an enormously profitable result for the Guggenheims, who ended up owning stock worth $45 million. This still stands as perhaps the most staggering single event in the history of the U.S. stock market.

When World War I broke out in 1914, M. Guggenheim and Sons had the capacity to efficiently and inexpensively produce nearly all the minerals and metals needed by the U.S. military. Always patriotic, Meyer was proud when all his grandchildren entered the armed services. While the younger generation fought in the field, Meyer and his sons worked on behalf of the war effort, selling liberty bonds, funding the Red Cross, and providing valuable advice to military leaders on how best to use America's mineral resources.

After the war, the Guggenheim family became interested in aviation. Meyer's grandson, Daniel Guggenheim, and his son, Harry, envisioned a day when people would routinely fly from one city to another. They donated money for all sorts of research into the possibilities of flight. Soon after Charles Lindbergh's historic solo flight across the Atlantic Ocean in 1927, the Daniel Guggenheim Fund was established to help build airports and new aeronautical companies throughout the United States.

Today, many different funds bearing the Guggenheim name dispense money to artists, scientists, and universities. But the most visible symbol of the Guggenheim's contribution to culture stands in New York City. The Solomon Guggenheim Museum is a spectacular building housing a magnificent collection of art. The gallery is several stories high, but because it is built on a spiral "corkscrew" plan, visitors may stroll through the collection without need of an elevator or stairway.

Meyer Guggenheim was always interested in making money, but his legacy helps fund many worthy endeavors that may not turn a financial profit. The Guggenheims, from Meyer to his great-great-grandchildren, have always seen it as their duty to return some of their good fortune to the community.

Alfred Stieglitz

PHOTOGRAPHER AND GALLERY OWNER
1864–1946

On a typical afternoon, Alfred Stieglitz listened to a group of students making fun of the art he had carefully hung on the walls of Gallery 291. The students giggled at a painting that seemed to be the work of a child. The woman depicted had two eyes on one side of her green face, and a nose pointing in the wrong direction! Stieglitz approached the group, adjusted his round glasses on his nose, and launched into a passionate defense of this masterpiece by a man named Pablo Picasso. "This artist," he declared, "is trying to express the way it truly feels to be human! Here is something new! This is the future of art in the United States," he told them.

Some left his gallery convinced, others believed the man was crazy. Today, it is clear that Stieglitz was a visionary, someone who could see in an instant which art would last and which would be forgotten. It takes a kind of courage to look at the work of an unknown artist and say it is good. Now we think of Matisse, Rodin, Picasso, and Georgia O'Keeffe as among the master artists. But there was a time when their new and strange work was scorned by all but a few. No single person did more to make the United States a home for modern art than Alfred Stieglitz.

Stieglitz himself was a magnificent artist, one of the world's greatest photographers. In many ways, he was responsible for establishing photography as an art form. In 1902, Stieglitz founded the Photo-Secession Group. Its members were dedicated to making photography into a "fine art." Until Stieglitz and his followers, most photographers simply recorded reality—landscapes, news stories, or portraits.

As a young man in Germany, Stieglitz had enrolled at Berlin Polytechnic with the intention of becoming an engineer. But then he happened to buy a small camera. He became so fascinated with photography's possibilities that he quit school to pursue photography on a full-time basis. Among Stieglitz's friends at this time were a few young painters. These artists did not take Alfred's new hobby seriously. Because a photograph could only record what was already there, they argued, the photographer was not a true artist. Stieglitz decided his goal would be to prove that photography had the potential to express emotions and not simply record the physical world.

Such goals were not taken lightly by Alfred Stieglitz. He was a scholarly young man, and very serious. Not content to simply walk about snapping pictures, he decided first to master all the technical aspects of photography. Only then, he reasoned, could he be a true spokesman for the new art form.

Not only did he learn existing techniques, he pioneered ideas of his own, many of which allowed one to make photographs in bad weather or in poor lighting. Also, he proved that small, handheld cameras could produce images comparable to those made with the huge, old-fashioned cameras that took hours to set up and used heavy plates. By 1910 (twenty years after he had returned to his native United States), his work began to win prizes and gain critical recognition.

All this work was done while Stieglitz was establishing perhaps the most important private art gallery in the history of the United States. Gallery 291, named for its street address, showed the newest work being created in the United States and throughout the world. Stieglitz believed America needed its own kind of art. In the early 1900s, American artists still imitated European masters. Stieglitz believed artists needed to use the vibrant energy of their own country to inspire them. After all, in the United States people were accomplishing feats of engineering and imagination beyond anything the Europeans had ever dreamed. Steel-framed skyscrapers rose into the skies, and new suspension bridges spanned vast waterways. Gallery 291 displayed works that Stieglitz believed embodied this new world. Many scoffed at his selections. Some people even got angry. They had never seen anything like this strange work he showed them. He ran several other galleries during his life, always striving to give struggling new artists a place to show their work. He also edited a magazine called *Camera Work* dedicated to new painting and photography. Today, issues of this magazine are prized by collectors as works of art in themselves.

Soon, Stieglitz was to meet the love of his life in Gallery 291. A friend gave him some drawings to look at. They were composed of simple lines and shading, not seeming to portray anything so much as different emotions. Stieglitz thought they were marvelously beautiful, capturing a "woman's soul on paper." He hung them on his walls immediately but could

Alfred Stieglitz visiting a show of paintings by his wife, the artist Georgia O'Keeffe

not quite remember the artist's name. He put up a sign saying the drawings were the work of Virginia O'Keeffe. A few days later, Georgia O'Keeffe stormed into the gallery demanding to know who had allowed him to hang her drawings. It was the beginning of an incredible relationship. The two were married in 1924, and their marriage was one of both emotional and artistic commitment. Stieglitz took more than 400 images of O'Keeffe during their time together, many of which were his most beautiful.

When Alfred Stieglitz died of heart failure in 1946, Georgia O'Keeffe and an assistant took several years sorting through his collection of art, and the thousands of letters sent to and received from many of the most important artists of the twentieth century. Stieglitz's influence on the art of the United States is hard to overestimate. Again and again, he discovered new artists, and made them famous. Stieglitz's own work was among the first photography to hang in the world's great museums. His magnificent photographs of O'Keeffe, along with his delicate studies of clouds, must be seen in person to be fully appreciated.

Lillian Wald

NURSE
1867–1940

Lillian Wald was born into a well-to-do Jewish family in Cincinnati, Ohio. Her father was a prosperous dealer in optical goods and Wald's childhood was happy. She later described herself as having been a "spoiled girl." She loved music and books and might easily have lived a comfortable life among family and friends. Instead, she devoted herself for more than forty years to helping the poor who suffered in crowded tenements on New York's Lower East Side.

While Lillian was still a girl, her older brother died. That event changed her forever. She resolved to do something worthwhile with her life. At the age of twenty-one, she wrote: "My life hitherto has been—I presume—a type of modern American young womanhood, days devoted to society, study, and housekeeping duties. . . . This does not satisfy me now. I feel the need of serious, definite work." Though it was unusual for proper young ladies of the time, Wald wanted to enroll in nursing school. She had been inspired by a dedicated nurse who came to care for an ailing sister. Wald's parents allowed her to attend a school of nursing in New York City beginning in 1889.

Upon graduation from nursing school, Wald went immediately to some of the poorest parts of New York. The crowded and unsanitary conditions of the Lower East Side created a breeding ground for terrible diseases such as tuberculosis and German measles. Wald knocked on doors, asking people if she could provide help. Her efforts soon gained the attention of Jewish-American financier and philanthropist Jacob Schiff. Schiff and his mother-in-law, Betty Solomon Loeb, contributed money toward establishing a nursing center in the area.

Wald and a friend from nursing school, Mary Maud Brewster, soon chose the old College Settlement House on Henry Street as the base of their operations and their home. They reasoned that it made sense for them to be residents of the neighborhood they intended to serve. In 1893, Jacob Schiff purchased the property and donated it to the two nurses. The place became the Henry Street Settlement House and provided a headquarters for the Visiting Nurse Service. By 1929, 250 nurses took part in the service. Wald envisioned a system of treatment that empowered poor people to help themselves. Treatment included lessons in nutrition, cleanliness, and the ability to resist unhealthy social conditions, such as drinking alcohol or gambling. In addition, Wald decided that those coming to the clinic would be charged a fee of ten cents so that they might retain their self-respect.

Wald ordered that the backyard of the Henry Street house be turned into a playground for children. Until then, not a single clean, safe, green space existed in the area where children could run and play. Believing such physical exercise essential to health and well-being, Wald helped found the Outdoor Recreation League in 1898. At the time, the idea of public parks and playgrounds was new and different.

Lillian Wald created other new and wonderful services. She established the first convalescent home for sick or injured women, children, and workers, as well as the first special education classes for children with disabilities.

Wald's ideas soon spread across the country, and public health nursing became a new profession. A tireless visionary, Wald made sure that her nurses examined every child in New York City's public school system, and she fought to establish a school lunch program to keep children from going hungry. In 1909, President Theodore Roosevelt commended her work and asked her to arrange a meeting to discuss the care of children in the United States. Wald lobbied the president and members of Congress to establish laws ending child labor.

Lillian Wald was also an early feminist. She angered some of Henry Street's contributors by speaking strongly in favor of voting rights for women. During World War I, she became president of the American Union Against Militarism. When the United States entered the war in 1917, this stance became unpopular and was considered by many to be unpatriotic. Though she believed war to be immoral on any grounds, Wald allowed the three buildings of Henry Street's Settlement House to be part of the war effort. She then suggested to President Woodrow Wilson that he name one of her nurses to direct the U.S. Army School for Nursing. Wilson agreed. During this time, Wald wrote a book about her experiences, *The House on Henry Street.*

Wald's father died in 1920, and her mother passed away in 1923. Wald took these losses hard, and perhaps succumbing to the stress, she suffered a heart attack from which she never fully recovered. In 1933, she resigned as head of the Henry Street Settlement House and retired to Westport, Connecticut, where she finished her second book, *Windows on Henry Street*. Lillian Wald died in 1940 after a long illness brought on by a cerebral hemorrhage. Her passing prompted an incredible outpouring of sadness and charity both in New York and across the nation.

It is interesting to note that although she was a Jewish American and much of her work was done among New York's immigrant Jewish community, Lillian Wald considered her efforts to be unconnected to her religion. Wald considered herself a humanitarian, doing all she could to help her fellow human beings. She brought kindness together with vision, hard work, and organizational skills, and she made social work and public nursing a joyous experience for those who worked with her.

Stephen S. Wise

INFLUENTIAL AMERICAN RABBI
1874–1949

Stephen Wise was the last in his family's long line of Hungarian rabbis. Educated in the public schools of Brooklyn and at Columbia University, he was trained as a rabbi by his father and other eminent scholars. As a young rabbi in New York City, Wise quickly became known as a brilliant public speaker. Even as a young man, his resonant baritone voice, large head, and strong facial features made him seem an ancient man of wisdom. But Wise was dissatisfied. Believing he had failed to "touch and kindle the hearts of people" in his congregation, he resigned his post in New York

City and took over a pulpit several thousand miles away, at Temple Beth Israel in Portland, Oregon.

Wise looked forward to a fresh start in Portland. He wanted to build a strong Jewish community in this new part of the United States. Here he would put into practice his belief that Judaism should be followed not only inside the temple, but in the outside world, as well. Jews, he believed, should become involved in community affairs, help the disadvantaged, and make strong political stands whenever justice and truth were threatened. He also wanted to help Jews improve relations with their Christian neighbors. Throughout his life, Wise enjoyed friendships with religious leaders of every faith.

In Oregon, Wise managed to "touch and kindle the hearts" of his flock. He and his congregation became well known throughout the Northwest for their involvement in projects to benefit the poor and their commitment to help politicians who supported social progress.

In 1906, Wise was offered the chance to take over the pulpit of Temple Emanu-El in New York City, the most prestigious post available to a rabbi in the United States. But the job came with a price. Wise could no longer speak out freely on any topic he wished. His desire to speak on behalf of exploited workers, for example, would have to be tempered out of respect for his wealthy temple members who owned large corporations. Wise was reminded by letter that "the pulpit should be subject to and under the control of the Board of Trustees." In response, Wise wrote an open letter to the board and temple members: "The chief office of a minister, I take it, is not to represent the views of the congregation, but to proclaim the truth as he sees it. . . . A free pulpit will sometimes stumble into error; a pulpit that is not free can never powerfully plead for truth and righteousness," he wrote. Wise turned down the job. He would not compromise in any way his ability to promote social justice from the pulpit.

Though he loved his work in the Pacific Northwest, in 1907 Wise fulfilled his dream of returning to New York and establishing a new congregation. Partly in response to Temple Emanu-El's attempt to muffle his voice, Wise wrote the following "principles" for his new congregation, called the Free Synagogue:

- Absolute Freedom of the Pulpit
- Abolition of distinction between rich and poor as to membership privileges
- Direct and full participation in all social services required by the community
- Complete identification not only with the Jewish faith, but with Israel's fate and future

Wise wrote a note to his wife in which he said, "The hardest year of my life is before me—and I hope the best. I have set out to do a great work. If only I have the strength to do it worthily." His congregation quickly grew from 50 members to 4,000, and services were held in Carnegie Hall. Many gentiles came to hear Wise speak on the important issues of the day. He spoke out about injustices in the steel industry, arguing for new and stricter labor laws to keep workers safe and help provide for their families. He attacked corrupt politicians. In one famous instance, he and a well-known Unitarian preacher named John Haynes Holmes drove a corrupt mayor out of office and into hiding in Europe.

During this time, Wise was deeply involved with the Zionist Organization of America and served several terms as its president. He believed that Jews needed a homeland. Soon, reports of the persecution of Europe's Jews during World War I (1914–18) strengthened his conviction. He spoke loudly in favor of making Palestine a new Jewish state. To organize such political efforts, Wise helped to establish the American Jewish Congress (AJC). The idea was to create a sort of governing body for American Jews that would examine, debate, and vote upon solutions to issues and problems. Wise believed this combined the ideal of democracy with the strong moral grounding of Judaism.

Besides fighting anti-Semitism throughout the world, the American Jewish Congress wielded political power within the United States. The AJC declared itself in favor of such ideas as public housing for the poor, establishment of the United Nations, and laws to protect children, the aged, and workers. Because the AJC represented more than two million voters, politicians were forced to listen to its concerns.

In 1922, in response to many requests from students, Wise founded the Jewish Institute of Religion, a school where rabbis were trained to see beyond the walls of the synagogue. They were trained to view their pulpits as a place from which to fight for truth and justice—for Jews and gentiles alike.

During the 1930s, as German dictator Adolf Hitler gained power in Europe, Wise tried to warn the U.S. government and society in general about Hitler. In 1933, Wise had told a group of ministers, "The racial fanaticism of the Hitler Reich may be a most immediate and deadly peril to us Jews, but it is no less truly a threat and a danger to all races and to all nations." His warnings proved prophetic. By the end of World War II in 1945, six million Jews had been murdered by Hitler and the Nazis. It took this ghastly crime to grant Wise his dream: Israel was founded in 1948 as a haven for Jewish survivors and refugees. But Wise's long fight to establish Israel, and the destruction of European Jewry, left him a melancholy and frail man.

On March 17, 1949, 1,200 guests attended Wise's seventy-fifth birthday. He died a month later. Remembered as one of the great shapers of modern Judaism, Stephen Wise worked always to push the religion forward, to make Judaism in a vital and positive force in everyday life. Wise devoted his life to public service, and was one of the most eloquent speakers on behalf of the oppressed everywhere that the world has known.

Harry Houdini

MAGICIAN AND ESCAPE ARTIST
1874–1926

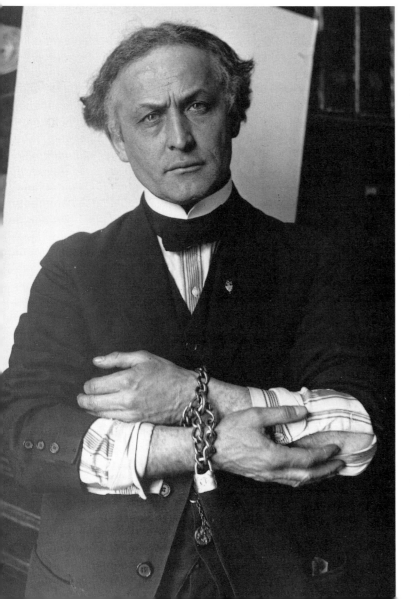

A crowd watches in awe as a heavily weighted packing crate is rolled onto a New York City dock. Harry Houdini stands aside, allowing members of the audience to inspect the crate and confirm that it is made of solid oak. A brass band bursts into song as a policeman steps forward to put manacles on Harry Houdini's feet and hands. Nodding to the cheering crowd, Houdini curls himself into the 2 by 2-foot (60 by 60-centimeter) box, which is then nailed shut and dumped by a crane into the Hudson River. The crowd gasps as the crate slowly sinks and air bubbles rise to the surface.

Thirty seconds pass......sixty seconds pass. The crowd is silent, becoming more and more nervous and excited with every passing second. Soon, one woman can bear the suspense no longer. She steps forward and screams, "Help him!" There are other calls for rescue. Houdini has now been underwater for more than two minutes. "For God's sake! He's drowning!" shouts a man in a bowler hat. Suddenly, as if on cue, Harry Houdini bursts from the dark water, smiling and waving his arms. The crowd roars with relief, and the band launches into "For He's a Jolly Good Fellow."

Harry Houdini performed stunts such as these hundreds of times, and they made him one of the most famous entertainers of his time. Houdini was born Ehrich Weiss in Budapest, Hungary. After his family moved to America, Ehrich grew up in Appleton, Wisconsin, where his father served as rabbi of a small Orthodox synagogue. Ehrich had no intention of following in his father's footsteps. He was fascinated by the circus and by performing. In 1882, at just nine years of age, he began working as "The Boy on the Flying Trapeze." Soon he began learning how to perform as a magician, and the great French magician Jean Eugène Robert-Houdin became his hero and inspiration. In honor of Robert-Houdin, Ehrich Weiss used Harry Houdini as his stage name. He called himself an "escapologist and magician."

In 1894, Houdini married Beatrice Rahner and trained her as his assistant. She was present for all his stunts when he began performing regularly at circuses and vaudeville shows. During these early days of his career, he once offered to sell the secrets of his various escapes to several New York newspapers for twenty dollars. They did not take him up on the offer. A few years later, he received offers as high as $100,000 for those same secrets. Houdini refused, and his secrets eventually died with him. To this day, many of his tricks and escapes cannot be explained by expert magicians.

When Harry Houdini toured Europe from 1900 to 1904, he was a smash hit. In Russia, his escape from an armored police van made him famous across that vast country. He amazed at least 100,000 British spectators when he escaped from a straitjacket while suspended upside down 25 feet (7.6 meters) in the air. Soon, Houdini was universally acclaimed as the "world's greatest magician." He appeared in several silent movies, which helped make him even more famous. In 1910, he even became a legendary aviator as the first person ever to fly a plane across the continent of Australia.

Houdini worked hard to keep himself in peak physical condition. He wanted to show the world that Jews were capable of magnificent physical, as well as intellectual, achievements. But his gifts were not only physical. Houdini was also a brilliant performer. In an age of great self-promoters like actress Sarah Bernhardt and circus showman P. T. Barnum, he made himself into the world's most famous person. He also never stopped working to improve in his craft. Everywhere he went he studied with locksmiths and fellow magicians. He became a master at dislocating his joints to allow escape from chains and straitjackets. He also learned to swallow keys and, once he was locked up, he would retrieve them by regurgitating them from his esophagus.

When his mother died in 1913, Houdini became obsessed with death. He had himself buried alive and dug his way out. He was fascinated by the spirit world and consulted with many spiritualists. Deciding all of them were fakes, he set about proving it and offered a huge reward to any psychic who could produce an effect he could not duplicate. No one was ever able to collect the money.

Even Houdini's death was strange and unlikely. He had always challenged fans to punch him in the stomach in order to prove how powerful his abdominal muscles were. But during one performance, an overzealous fan

Harry Houdini is bound in a straightjacket in preparation for a 1915 escape stunt.

hit Houdini before he was ready, causing internal injuries. Houdini then died trying to escape from a sealed tank of water. His death occurred on Halloween night, 1926.

Houdini and his wife had agreed on a number of "signs" he could give after his death to reveal he had entered the "spirit world." No such signs were ever received by his wife. Houdini's funeral was attended by luminaries from entertainment, business, and government. Charlie Chaplin and Rudolph Valentino, among others, spoke at the service. Houdini's incredible feats, along with his strange and untimely death, make him a unique character in Jewish-American history.

Al Jolson

SINGER AND ENTERTAINER
1886–1950

The *Jazz Singer* was the biggest hit movie of 1927. It told the story of Al Jolson, born Asa Yoelson in Lithuania. At the time of the film, the real Al Jolson was still a relatively young man, but he was already a legend, without question the most popular entertainer of his time.

As the movie revealed, Jolson was the son of a cantor, a position of great honor in the Jewish religion. The cantor sings during religious services. Cantors, like rabbis, often pass down their skills from generation to generation, and Jolson's father was no exception. He trained his two sons to follow in his footsteps. But being a cantor was not always a profitable profession. The Yoelsons traveled all over Russia looking for work, always on the verge of starving. Tired of such trials, they decided to emigrate to the United States in 1894. Upon arrival in New York City, the name Asa Yoelson became "Americanized" to Al Jolson.

When Al was just ten years old, his mother died, and he decided to set out on his own rather than stay with his strict father. He was tired of his father's demands. Though he loved to perform, Al had little interest in becoming a cantor. He wanted to sing for a broader audience. His brother Harry felt the same way. Soon, the two ran away from home, believing they would work hard and become rich and famous. While living on his own, Jolson met and became friends with many African-American performers. He loved the songs they sang and the way they sang them. Their music was often deeply spiritual, sung with strong emotion and drama. He decided to base his act on the music and performers he loved.

Jolson went so far as to sing in what was called "blackface" by covering his face in dark greasepaint. White gloves completed his costume. Today, for a Caucasian performer to dress up as an African-American in this way would be highly offensive, but in the early 1900s, such stylized performance was acceptable. And Jolson did it better than anyone. Appearing mostly in variety shows called vaudeville, he sang many of the songs his African-American friends had taught him. Before Jolson sang them, such songs had rarely been heard by white audiences.

Soon, Jolson developed the habit of dropping to one knee and crooning with his arms outspread and face lifted to the bright lights. Some who knew Jolson claim he began performing on one knee when an infection in his leg made it painful to stand. Whatever the case may be, it became one of his trademarks.

By 1906, Jolson had some success with New York audiences. But it was

Al Jolson wore the traditional "blackface" makeup of minstrel shows in the historic movie The Jazz Singer.

not until he took the long train ride to San Francisco that he began to gain a national reputation. In San Francisco, he sang to sold-out theaters night after night, and his heartfelt rendition of the George Gershwin song "Swanee" became a huge hit. Audiences roared at his jokes and wept when he sang sad songs. Something in his face and the way he moved made people react however he wished. It was a kind of magic. Every night, the applause was thunderous. "All right! All right, folks," Jolson grinned one night, "You ain't heard nothin' yet!" The audience roared again, and the saying became yet another Jolson trademark.

When he returned to New York, Jolson became the biggest hit ever on the Broadway stage. When he released a record album of old favorite songs, it sold a million copies, an unheard of number seventy-five years ago. Jolson soon added a successful film career to his list of accomplishments. In 1927, he starred in *The Jazz Singer,* a landmark movie in that it was the first "talking picture"—the first movie with sound. The film not only launched a new era in American entertainment, but it made Jolson the most famous singer in the world.

Jolson's career spanned from the vaudeville era into the 1950s. Upon returning from a trip to entertain U.S. troops in the Korean War, he collapsed and died of a heart attack at age 64. Jolson left most of his $4 million estate to be divided equally between Jewish, Catholic, and Protestant charities. When Al Jolson performed songs he made them his own. Songs like "Swanee," "Danny Boy," and "Mammy" can hardly be sung today without imitating Al Jolson's dramatic, full-throated delivery.

Irving Berlin

POPULAR COMPOSER
1888–1989

Did you know that the man who wrote "White Christmas" was Jewish? Surely, he learned nothing about Christmas from his father—a rabbi and cantor. Despite being born into poverty and having no formal musical training, Irving Berlin became the most popular songwriter the United States has ever produced.

In the late 1800s, Irving Berlin was a poor boy living in a tiny Jewish town near the Siberian border. At this time, his name was Israel Baline. The Baline family suffered under harsh Russian rule. Soldiers raided Jewish villages, vandalizing property, burning down houses, beating the villagers and worse. Such raids, called "pogroms," sent many Russian and Polish Jews to the United States in hopes of a better future. The Balines became one of these poor refugee families. But the United States did not provide immediate relief from their poverty. Two years after they arrived, Israel's father died, and the eight-year-old boy sang on New York street corners for a few pennies to help his family. When he was fourteen, he ran away from home, spending his days with down-and-out musicians in New York's tough Bowery district. It was here that Israel Baline discovered his love of music.

Izzie, as he was now called, soon taught himself how to play the piano. He ended up knowing only how to play the black keys, and he never learned to read written music. In fact, long after he was famous he had a special piano built that allowed him to play any song in F-sharp, the only key he ever mastered.

In 1907, while working as a singing waiter in a Chinatown restaurant, he and another pianist wrote a song called "Marie from Sunny Italy." It took four years of going door to door from one music publisher to another, but eventually Israel Baline sold the song. "Marie from Sunny Italy" was Izzie's first hit. Soon after, a publisher misspelled his name on a piece of sheet music and he became Irving Berlin.

In those days, most middle-class families owned a piano. For entertainment, parents and children played and sang together, so there was a huge demand for catchy tunes on sheet music. In 1911, Irving Berlin wrote a song called "Alexander's Ragtime Band" that was easy to sing and had bouncy words that made people happy. It sold more than a million copies of sheet music. This was only the first time Berlin would give the people exactly what they wanted. He made $100,000 from the song and became an instant sensation.

Berlin then discovered and took over the world of musical theater with

Irving Berlin composed dozens of famous American songs.

hit Broadway shows like *Watch Your Step* in 1914 and *Century Girl* two years later. He was a smash in Hollywood, too. In 1935, he wrote the score for Fred Astaire and Ginger Roger's most famous movie, *Top Hat*. Decade after decade, Berlin remained the top songwriter in the United States. His simple but poetic lyrics and strong melodies expressed emotions felt by everyone. The happiness and sorrow of being in love was a constant theme. Well into his seventies, he continued to write music loved by every generation. In 1946, more than fifty years after his first hit, he was still the most popular composer in the country. The 1946 version of his show *Annie Get Your Gun,* included such legendary songs as "There's No Business Like Show Business" sung by Ethel Merman.

Berlin also was known for his patriotic odes to his adopted homeland. "God Bless America" became one of the nation's favorite songs, and Berlin donated all of the proceeds, more than $500,000, to the Girl Scouts and Boy Scouts of America. He also wrote a number of shows to entertain the troops during World War II. *This Is the Army* earned almost $10 million, all of which he donated to Army Emergency Relief.

And what about "White Christmas"? How is it that one of the most heart-felt Christmas songs was written by a Jewish American? Well, despite his strict Jewish upbringing, Irving Berlin had been in love with the warm spirit of Christmas since childhood. As a child, he would often sneak out of his house and visit his Irish neighbors to look at their Christmas tree.

Today, "White Christmas," as well as such Berlin songs like "Always," "Blue Skies," "Easter Parade," and "Cheek to Cheek," are so-called standards—tunes that must be in the repertoire of any young jazz musician hoping to play with other musicians. One hears his influence even in songs by The Beatles, Elton John, Billy Joel, and countless others. During his long life, Berlin wrote more than 900 songs. He remained healthy and sharp-minded even through his 100th birthday. As Jerome Kern, another great American composer, once said, "Irving Berlin has no place in American popular music, he is American popular music."

The Jews Who Created Hollywood

At the turn of the century, movies were seen mainly in penny arcades and small theaters at amusement parks. Respectable Christian gentlemen did not operate such tawdry businesses. This created an opportunity for eager Jewish businessmen who were turned away by more established industries, such as banking and manufacturing. So in the early 1900s, a number of Jewish immigrants from Eastern Europe quit selling fish, gloves, or scrap metal and got into the penny arcade business.

As a result, many Jews entered the movie business almost by accident. Around this time, Thomas Edison's kinetoscope and other coin-operated moving-picture viewers began raking in profits. The public loved movies, and soon penny arcade operaters opened special theaters that used projection to show films on large screens. These theaters grew more and more plush and comfortable as the American appetite for films increased. And a boom in theaters meant a need for more movies.

The first movie "moguls" (the leaders of the industry) were mostly uneducated Eastern European Jews who owned theaters and needed more cheap movies to show. A few of these theater owners began producing their own films to avoid paying for movies made by others. When these businessmen invested money in the making of a film, they did not care whether it was artistic. They just wanted to sell tickets. Many modern movies are still made with the same idea. A movie was—and is—very expensive to produce, so most filmmakers want to appeal to the broadest possible audience.

The first of the Jewish-American moviemakers to become a millionaire was **Adolph Zukor (1873–1976).** Zukor emigrated from Hungary to the United States in 1888 and began his working life sweeping floors. He was ambitious and soon became a successful furrier. In 1903, Zukor convinced a fellow furrier, Marcus Loew, to invest in penny arcades. The gamble soon bloomed into the Loew Company, which owned a number of theaters and began to make movies to show in them. Most movies of the time were "shorts" lasting ten or fifteen minutes. Zukor believed the movie-going public wanted evening-length entertainment and began making feature films. He was soon proven correct.

Zukor also recognized that when the novelty of movies wore off, audiences would pay to see their favorite actors or actresses in films. He helped create the idea of "movie stars" with his Famous Players in Famous Plays company of actors, which included Mary Pickford. Until she was signed by Zukor, she was referred to only as "Little Mary." The public did not even know her name. But when Zukor signed Mary Pickford to a huge contract, he built her into Hollywood's first major star. Zukor enlarged his kingdom by absorbing other movie companies. He bought Paramount, a movie-distribution company, and made it the biggest production studio in the industry. Paramount established a policy that required theater owners to show all of Paramount's films—fifty-two weekly shows per year. This guaranteed that all the movies Paramount produced would earn money. Such "block booking" prevented theater owners from picking only the best movies to exhibit and guaranteed profits for Zukor and his investors. The practice

Louis B. Mayer was one of the great Hollywood moguls.

soon became an industry standard.

Zukor's partner at Paramount, **Jesse Lasky (1880–1958),** was an experienced theatrical man and hired many of the greatest actors of the day. Pickford, Rudolph Valentino, Gloria Swanson, the Marx Brothers, Bing Crosby, and Cary Grant were just a few of the stars Lasky discovered and signed in his fifteen years at Paramount.

During the 1920s, Metro-Goldwyn-Mayer (MGM) rose to become a powerful studio. Marcus Loew, Zukor's former partner, owned hundreds of theaters nationwide and wanted to show his own films in his theaters. So he bought the nearly bankrupt Metro Picture Company and the struggling Goldwyn Picture Company. Loew put **Louis B. Mayer (1885–1957),** a fellow theater owner, in charge of produc-

A 1905 photo of Warner brothers Sam and Jack (left), posing before an Atlantic City, New Jersey, theater where their motion pictures were shown.

tion. Mayer's motto was "great star, great director, great play, great cast." MGM became known for its high-quality family entertainment. Much of the credit for MGM's success belonged to Mayer's assistant, **Irving Thalberg (1899–1936).** Thalberg worked tirelessly to ensure that every aspect of a film's production—from script writing to costumes—met the highest standards.

The four **Warner** brothers—**Harry (1881–1958), Albert (1884–1967), Sam (1888–1927),** and **Jack (1892–1978)**—began their careers as salesmen before turning to motion pictures. They produced tougher, more violent and realistic films than MGM. Their stars included James Cagney and

Bette Davis. Warner Brothers also led the way in animation, giving us Bugs Bunny, Porky Pig, and Elmer Fudd. Most significantly, the Warners released the first full-length movie with sound, *The Jazz Singer,* in 1927.

Other Jewish Americans important to the early days of Hollywood included **William Fox (1879–1952),** who built Fox Film Corporation with stars like cowboy Tom Mix and exotic beauty Theda Bara. In 1939, **David O. Selznik (1902–1965)** produced *Gone With the Wind,* which today is still considered one of Hollywood's greatest films. Selznik is said to have designed every shot of the movie, and he spent the rest of his life trying to top this blockbuster. **Samuel Goldwyn (1882–1974)** became an independent producer and was responsible for a number of classic films. He hired actors like Gary Cooper, David Niven, and some of the greatest comics in the movies.

All of these movie moguls were Jewish Americans. In fact, there were very few early Hollywood power brokers who were *not* Jewish. Some of Hollywood's Jewish elite remained committed to Judaism throughout their lives, while others aggressively attempted to shake off their Jewish heritage. They believed that their Jewishness stood in the way of success in the United States, and they assimilated themselves into American culture as they created the very medium that began to define that culture.

In addition to the moguls who ran Hollywood, countless other Jewish-American executives, actors, writers, and directors worked for them. Together, they made Hollywood, California, one of the most famous spots on the planet.

Groucho Marx

COMEDIAN
1890–1977

Minnie Marx thought her five sons were hilariously funny. As she watched them grow up, she was sure they would become famous. As young men, they searched for an "act"—just the right style of comedy and music that would ring true with audiences.

Groucho Marx and his brothers emerged from a tradition called vaudeville. Before radio and movies became the main sources of entertainment in the United States, local theater's presented variety shows that included comedians, singers, musicians, tap dancers, and animal acts. Conditions were not always ideal for these performers. Audiences were sometimes drunk and disorderly, or just plain bored. Because of such difficulties, successful vaudevillians became unflappable professionals who knew how to deliver exactly the entertainment people wanted.

Describing the Marx Brothers' comedy is impossible—like describing a dance, or a symphony. One must see it and hear it to understand its comic genius. The core of the group consisted of Groucho, with his big cigar and painted mustache; Chico, with his funny hat and ridiculous accent; and silent Harpo, with his curly hair, bulging eyeballs, and bicycle horn. Together, they created some of the funniest moments in movie history. Historians point out that the Marx Brothers' humor was based mostly on problems in communication—with Groucho's confusing logic, Chico's accent, and Harpo's mute clowning. Often they were all talking at once, and nobody was listening. This was a hilarious send-up of daily life in the ethnically mixed inner-city neighborhoods where most immigrant Jews lived, and although their jokes were never based on "Jewish" subjects, their style of humor was decidedly "Jewish."

Groucho Marx is idolized today for his brilliant comic mind and larger-than-life personality. He had wanted to be admired as a doctor but dropped out of grammar school and became a singer and performer instead. For fifteen years, the Marx Brothers honed their skills on the stage. Gradually, they adopted distinct personalities. Groucho was the ringleader, a wise guy who talked circles around anyone who got in his way, insulting respectable citizens so quickly they didn't know what hit them. The brothers' 1924 show *I'll Say She Is* was a hit across the country, but Groucho was hesitant to do the show on Broadway. He thought New York City critics would hate the show's silliness and would be merciless in their reviews. Groucho was wrong. The famous critic Alexander Wolcott thought the show was hilarious. He asked his readers to "take it on faith from one who, at [the show's]

The Marx Brothers (left to right): Groucho, Harpo, and Chico

conclusion had to be picked up out of the aisle and placed gently back in his seat."

A Marx Brothers' play was never the same from one night to the next, as the brothers constantly added their own jokes. One story describes a night when famous Jewish-American playwright George S. Kaufman, who wrote for the Marx Brothers several times, stood in the wings during a performance. Suddenly he hushed those around him: "Quiet!" he demanded. "I think I just heard one of my original lines!"

Soon, Hollywood recognized a chance to sell some movie tickets. Among their most famous movies were *Animal Crackers* (1930) and *A Night at the Opera* (1935)—their biggest hit and Groucho's favorite of all their films. *Duck Soup* (1933) was a political satire in which Groucho played Rufus T. Firefly, leader of a mythical country named Fredonia. Today, it is considered one of the great comedies of all time. Once they hit Hollywood, the Marx Brothers became even more famous than they were as stage comedians.

Groucho was the true genius among his brothers. When informed he would not be allowed to join a certain country club because he was Jewish, Groucho Marx quipped, "That's OK. I refuse to join any club that would have me as a member." After their stage and film careers had ended, Groucho Marx remained nationally prominent. He hosted his own radio and television program, *You Bet Your Life,* for ten years. Groucho influenced all the comedians who followed him, and his humor became especially popular in the 1960s. People who were eager for social change loved the way Groucho flouted authority and made fun of those in charge of the world. Today, Groucho remains extremely popular and immediately recognizable. His face even adorns a U.S. postage stamp. He died in 1977 at the age of 87.

Jack Benny

COMEDIAN
1894 – 1974

Hold-Up Man: *Your money or your life!*

Silence.

Hold-Up Man: *C'mon, bud!*

Jack Benny: *...I'm thiiinking it over!*

J ack Benny was so good at playing a vain, pompous miser that many came to believe he really was the fictional character he created. Actually, the opposite was true. He was a generous unassuming man, loved by those who knew him. Benny became famous on the radio during the 1930s and remained a huge star until his death in 1974. It was his incredible comic timing, allowing listeners' imaginations to run wild during his perfectly placed pauses, for which he is best remembered. Benny's character absorbed insults with a long pause followed by an unexplainably hilarious, "Well!" *The Jack Benny Show* was a hit on its first broadcast in 1932 on David Sarnoff's NBC radio network, and it remained at or near the top of the ratings until 1950, when it became a hit on television. Now viewers could see what went on during all those pauses, and they laughed even harder. Benny was masterful in his reaction to an insult or bad situation, placing his chin in his hand and turning to the audience with a look of utter dismay.

Jack Benny was born Benjamin Kubelsky. Waukegan, Illinois, his hometown, became a subject of his running gags. Benny truly enjoyed people and always wanted to be a performer. By age 17, he was on the road working in vaudeville shows, playing his violin and cracking jokes. His act did not really become popular until he entered the navy in World War I. During the long and boring hours on board ship and in the barracks, Benny tested comic material on his fellow sailors and worked up a new act. Benny's most famous gag involved his violin. He always apologized for his terrible playing, then played anyway—a sickly version of the ballad "Love in Bloom." Again, it was the pained look on Benny's face when he hit a sour note that made the joke funny for fifty years. And it was that same expression that landed him the radio show where he took on the character of an aging bachelor and mean-spirited miser.

Benny was extremely loyal to those who worked for him on the show, retaining the same crew of comedians and musicians throughout his long career. The woman who played his girlfriend on the show was actually his wife, Mary Livingstone. Eddie Anderson played Benny's gravel-voiced African-American valet, Rochester. Mel Blanc, who would later become the voice of Bugs Bunny and many other cartoon characters, got his start on

Benny's show. Countless young performers learned the art of comic timing listening to and watching Jack Benny. Many libraries have audio tapes of *The Jack Benny Show,* a cornerstone of what is now considered radio's "Golden Age."

Jack Benny worked on behalf of various Jewish charities, contributing generous sums of his money and his time. When he died in 1974 at the age of eighty, the entire entertainment industry mourned his passing. Benny's peers honored him as a true artist.

George Gershwin

COMPOSER
1898–1937

Ore day in 1924, George Gershwin boarded a train, a journey that turned out to be one of the most important in the history of American music. Gershwin took his seat and soon began listening to the rhythm of the wheels as they clicked along the tracks. He closed his eyes. In his mind, he heard the beginnings of what would become *Rhapsody in Blue,* his best-known symphonic piece. *Rhapsody in Blue* brought together and truly blended American jazz and European classical music. From the snaking clarinet that opens the piece, audiences were swept away. It was

George Gershwin, along with fellow composer Duke Ellington, who brought the art of jazz from nightclubs into the concert hall.

Gershwin was born Jacob Gershowitz in Brooklyn, but later changed his name to sound "less Jewish." This was common practice among Jewish entertainers who wanted to become a hit with a mainly gentile public. When Jacob was nine years old, his father bought a piano so that his older brother, Ira, could learn to play. But Ira was bookish and shy, more interested in writing poetry than performing on piano. So it was Jacob who ended up mastering the piano while Ira continued to work with words. As an adult, Ira would write the words to most of his younger brother's best songs.

In his teens, George Gershwin was a good enough pianist and singer that he got a job in New York "pounding songs." A song pounder sat at a piano in the lobby of a music publisher playing and singing the company's newest offerings. Members of the public were invited to stop by and listen. The experience taught Gershwin a lot about the music that touched people. But he soon tired of the job and applied for the position of musical secretary to his idol, Irving Berlin. After auditioning for the job, Berlin's manager told him he was too good for such work. "Go write songs of your own," he was told. So he did.

In 1920, Al Jolson made Gershwin's "Swanee" into a huge hit. Gershwin's output of beloved tunes never slowed down from there. His songs featured strong rhythms, catchy melodies, and Ira's witty lyrics. Always ambitious, Gershwin began to move beyond writing single tunes and composed an opera called *Blue Monday* in 1922. Though the piece was not completely successful, its composition taught Gershwin lessons he put to use in *Rhapsody in Blue* two years later. Following that success, he wrote perhaps his most musically important piece, *Concerto in F*. Many experts believe this to be the best classical music ever written in the United States. In

1928, Gershwin finished *An American in Paris,* a tone poem that captured the bustle and romance of the French capital.

Throughout the 1920s, George worked with Ira to produce some of the world's best popular music. They wrote a string of Broadway hits, including *Lady Be Good* and *Funny Face,* performed by dancers Fred and Adele Astaire. Their 1931 musical *Of Thee I Sing* won them the Pulitzer Prize for Drama, an award never before given to a musical show. In 1935, they produced their masterpiece, *Porgy and Bess.* At the time, however, the show was not a hit. It was a stark and fairly realistic portrait of African-Americans living in the Bayou of Louisiana. *Porgy and Bess* startled audiences that were accustomed to light musical comedy, not raw human emotion, suffering, love, and rage.

Tragically, George Gershwin died of brain cancer in 1937, when he was only thirty-eight years old. The millions who love his music are left to wonder what he might have produced had he lived even another decade. Incorporating such diverse styles as African-American spirituals, Jewish religious singing, ragtime, swing jazz, and classical, Gershwin took full advantage of the rich musical variety found in the United States. Today, songs like "Lady Be Good," "Fascinating Rhythm," "The Man I Love," "Strike Up the Band," and "Embraceable You" still sound fresh, and are still included among the most basic tunes every jazz singer and musician must know.

Jewish Gangsters

As immigrants poured into the United States around the turn of the century, cities became unofficially divided into various ethnic neighborhoods. The Lower East Side of New York, for example, was predominantly Jewish, and it bordered Little Italy, which was filled with Italian immigrants. Within each neighborhood, American newcomers struggled to create their new lives. For the most part, different ethnic groups got along with one another. But, inevitably, disputes occurred and sometimes erupted into fights. In each ethnic group, battles were fought by young men who formed gangs. Later on, these alliances often became criminal operations.

Each community had its share of such criminals. Jewish gangs at the turn of the century served mainly to protect law-abiding Jews against rival gangs from other neighborhoods, or against violent anti-Semites who sometimes attacked innocent Jews. Legend has it, for instance, that gangster "Nails" Morton saw to it that the young and frail Benny Goodman could safely pass through Polish neighborhoods on his way to a daily clarinet lesson at Chicago's Hull House.

Most American Jews denied the existence of Jewish gangs. Peaceful immigrants desired no visible connection with those who lived outside the law. The appearance that a given ethnic group was lawless might stop further immigration. So Jews often grew angry when another Jew admitted the presence of Jewish gangs. *"A shonder fer de goyim!"* they would say in Yiddish. ("We can talk about it among ourselves, but don't let the gentiles find out!")

The most feared, violent, and profitable of Jewish gangs grew up from boyhood friendships formed on New York's Lower East Side. The alliance between **Meyer Lansky (1902–1983)** and **Benjamin "Bugsy" Siegel (1906–1947)** led to the "Bugs and Meyer Mob." While still teenagers, the two organized illegal dice games, stole cars, and intimidated store owners for "protection" money. They eventually met up with **Arnold Rothstein (1882–1928),** another Jewish immigrant and the most prominent criminal mind of his time. Between 1915 and 1928, Rothstein controlled illegal gambling in most of the United States and paid off police officials and judges to maintain his power. Part of Rothstein's genius was the care with which he maintained his respectable image. Despite the fact that he was a criminal (and he was a Jew), he enjoyed friendships with politicians, sports and movie stars, and important people in the legitimate business world.

Rothstein taught Lansky, Siegel, and their friends to act respectably in order to distance themselves from their criminal activities. Gangster Lucky Luciano remembered, "Rothstein taught me how to dress and behave in public. . . . He taught me how to use knives and forks and things like that at the dinner table. . . . He was the best etiquette teacher a guy could have." The ability to behave in a non-threatening manner allowed gangsters to stay out of newspapers and avoid public outrage, which might lead to a police crackdown.

Rothstein not only controlled gambling, he often "fixed" the results of sporting events so that he could place large bets and be certain of the outcome. His most famous fix was the 1919 World Series. Rothstein and his associates paid, or promised to pay, several thousand dollars to eight members of a great Chicago White Sox team. In exchange, the players inten-

Bugsy Siegel (left) and Meyer Lansky (right) were two of the most notorious gangsters in American history.

tionally played poorly, and Chicago lost to a weaker Cincinnati Reds team. After the scheme was discovered, the eight White Sox were banned from baseball for life, but Rothstein was never indicted in the scandal. He was gunned down in a hotel lobby nine years later in a dispute over a bad debt.

Following Rothstein's assassination, Meyer Lansky soon became the most powerful gangster in the United States. He and Bugsy Siegel made a fortune in "bootlegging"—manufacturing and selling liquor illegally during the 1930s, when alcoholic beverages were outlawed. Soon, the two decided they needed more muscle to enforce their hold on such illegal operations.

Another boyhood friend from the neighborhood, Lepke Buchalter, formed what became known as Murder Inc. Buchalter and his thugs committed acts of terror and violence against enemies of the Bugs and Meyer Mob. Murder Inc. also worked as paid assassins. By 1934, Lansky was able to consolidate power when most of the country's crime leaders agreed to a cease-fire and formed a loose federation dedicated to getting rich from gambling, prostitution, bootlegging, and narcotics.

Lansky's evil genius was to operate his illegal enterprises as a business. He made his decisions based solely on practical considerations, not on revenge or issues of ethnic pride. In this way, he eliminated much friction between Jews, Italians, Poles, and others involved in the business of crime. Such relative peace left more time for making money. Lansky was a small and quiet man who dressed well and showed no tendency toward violence. Even an agent with the Federal Bureau of Investigation marveled at Lansky's abilities: "He would have been chairman of the board of General Motors if he'd gone into legitimate business."

Bugsy Siegel lacked Lansky's discipline and professionalism. In fact, Siegel earned the nickname "Bugs" from those who witnessed his violent fits of temper. Few called him "Bugs" or "Bugsy" to his face, as he sometimes shot those who dared. During the 1930s, Siegel traveled to California and was put in charge of the mob's West Coast operations. A handsome, charming man who was always well dressed, Siegel soon became a popular guest at Hollywood parties. He was friendly with many of the biggest movie stars, including Jean Harlow, Clark Gable, and Cary Grant.

After World War II, the mob enjoyed even more financial success, and Siegel began dreaming of a legal gambling oasis in the desert north of California. Using vast amounts of the mob's cash, he built and opened the Flamingo Hotel in Las Vegas, Nevada, in 1945. People thought he was crazy—at that time Las Vegas was a dusty, boring place in the middle of nowhere. Siegel's vision of Las Vegas as a huge and bustling entertainment hub eventually came true, but he did not live to see it. It is believed that when Meyer Lansky learned that Siegel was stealing money from the casino, Lansky ordered his boyhood friend's murder.

Meyer Lansky was one of the few important gangsters not to die violently. By 1970, he controlled an estimated $300 million worth of casinos and hundreds of other operations, both legal and illegal, throughout the United States and the Bahamas. That year, fearing he would soon be arrested on charges of income tax evasion, Lansky fled to Israel. After several years, the Israeli government agreed to send him back to the United States to stand trial. By then, however, Lansky was an old man sick with lung cancer. He died in Miami and was buried in an Orthodox Jewish cemetery.

What had begun as a means of self-protection and small-time profit in the streets of New York, Chicago, and Detroit ended up a multibillion-dollar crime syndicate. During the 1970s, the FBI did much to destroy Jewish and Italian gangs. Today, although Jewish gangsters continue to operate, none enjoy the sweeping power of Rothstein, Lansky, Siegel, Buchalter, and others between 1910 and 1970. Though far from being heroes, such criminals were a fascinating, yet repellent, aspect of Jewish life in the United States.

Louise Nevelson

SCULPTOR
1899–1988

Louise Nevelson was married young and soon gave birth to a baby boy. At first, she was happy in her life as a wife and mother in New York. But her husband did not understand her dream of being an artist too. He resented that she came home late from the Art Students League, where she took classes in dance and sculpture. She loved to spend hours there talking with other artists, while he wanted her home preparing his dinner. Soon, Nevelson made the difficult choice to leave her husband and child behind to pursue her career. In 1931, she went to Germany to study with Hans Hoffman, a famous art teacher.

Her family was not terribly surprised. They knew Louise was strong-minded and would not accept being told what to do and when to do it. But they always thought she would be a singer or dancer. In some ways though, it makes sense that she became a sculptor. Her father ran a successful lumber business. As a child, she had spent a great deal of time around wood and people who built things with it. As her career as a sculptor progressed, she worked with many materials—clay, marble, even aluminum—but her greatest work was made with wood.

Nevelson's journey to Germany was badly timed. Adolf Hitler was coming to power, and Hans Hoffman and Nevelson (both Jews) were forced to flee the German government's anti-Semitic policies. Nevelson went to Vienna and then to Paris, where she visited the Musée de l'Homme. The museum housed a collection of African sculpture. The strong, simple figures carved out of wood made a lasting impression on Nevelson. She vowed to bring such simplicity and strength to her own work.

Nevelson's artistic career began to truly take shape when she assisted artist Diego Rivera on a series of huge murals. The work covered the massive, high walls of the Rockefeller Center lobby in New York City. Rivera's interests as an artist were very different from Nevelson's. He painted images of people, often peasants, engaged in daily life. His goal was political, to show the strength and nobility of farmers, workers, and the poor. Though his style was nothing like her own, Nevelson devoted herself completely to working on the murals and helped to convert Rivera's sketches into huge paintings. She found the job tedious, but educational. Also, she developed a close friendship with Rivera and his wife, which lasted most of her life.

In 1936, Nevelson presented her own sculpture at a formal show. A *New York Times* critic wrote that he especially liked the way she used color and mixed three-dimensional forms with two-dimensional collage. Her show's success was a great relief to Nevelson. She had worried she did not have the

A 1958 sculpture by Louise Nevelson titled Sky Cathedral

talent to become a serious artist, and that she had risked too much by giving up her husband and son.

The 1930s were a difficult time in the United States, especially for artists. In the midst of the Great Depression, the economy was in a shambles and many people had trouble making a living. Art seemed an unaffordable luxury. Soon, the U.S. government created many programs to help artists and others survive. One such program was the Works Progress Administration (WPA). Nevelson taught sculpture classes for the WPA to make a living while she worked hard on her own pieces. Many of the sculptures were plaster molds that were supposed to yield bronze statues. But Nevelson could not afford to have such castings made. She moved often during this period and discarded most of her work each time she took a new apartment. Putting her hard work in the trash was difficult for her, but it also helped her grow as an artist. She was always working on something totally new.

In the 1940s, she at last discovered the kind of sculptures she most wanted to make. She created huge walls made of wooden boxes. She then placed various objects she had found in the boxes—everything from a piece of rusted metal to an old clock. She began collecting wood of all sorts from the trash, lumber yards, even from old furniture. She called these huge works "environments" and many consisted of several walls so as to create the effect of being their own small room.

As Nevelson became more sure of what she needed to do to succeed, more of her friends began to see her as a little bit crazy. Her home in New York became her "gold" studio. Here she made huge sculptures that were all painted gold, as well as collages of found objects called "assemblages." A second studio was her "white" studio, and a third was devoted solely to black sculpture. Nevelson spent thirteen years creating one massive black environment, which she called "Mrs. N's Palace." For the Federal Courthouse in Philadelphia, she created a black wall to commemorate those killed in the Holocaust. Her work can also be seen today in the Louise Nevelson Plaza near New York City's financial district. In her later years, Nevelson became a highly respected spokesperson on the value and importance of art in the United States and served on a number of boards and committees devoted to helping young artists. Louise Nevelson died in 1988 when she was eighty-nine years old.

Hyman G. Rickover

REAR ADMIRAL OF THE U.S. NAVY
1900–1986

As a military man, Hyman Rickover envisioned and helped create nuclear-powered submarines. But he also spoke out strongly on the need for improved educational opportunities in the United States and against wasteful military spending. Ultimately, he called for nuclear disarmament.

Rickover was, by all accounts, a difficult person to get along with. A stubborn man, he was convinced he knew more than almost anyone around him, and he did not care what others thought of him. Even as a boy, he had few friends and was more interested in reading and studying than in playing with other children. His father made little money, and the family was always in danger of slipping into poverty. Rickover came to like living efficiently, without luxury or waste. Even as an admiral with a hefty salary, he continued his frugal boyhood habits.

Upon high school graduation, all of Rickover's reading and studying paid off when a local congressman sponsored his application to the prestigious U.S. Naval Academy in Annapolis, Maryland.

As payment for receiving training at the academy, each cadet is required to serve in the navy for five years. When he entered the service, Rickover had no intention of staying longer than the five years he owed the country for his college education. Then he planned to get a higher-paying job to help his family. However, after graduation in 1922, Rickover spent five years at sea and realized he truly loved the navy. And the more he thought about his years at Annapolis, the more he believed he owed his country. So Rickover remained in the navy and studied electrical engineering and submarine science. He gradually rose through the ranks. Not considered a truly exceptional officer by those who found him difficult to work with, he was sharp-witted, spoke his mind, and could be counted on to accomplish whatever he promised to do. In 1937, he was named a commander in the Philippines.

In 1939, with World War II brewing in Europe, Rickover returned to the United States, where he headed the electrical section of the Bureau of Ships in Washington, D.C. There he learned how slow and tangled the navy's bureaucracy could be. Getting anything done required too much paperwork, so he regularly skirted regulations to speed operations and taught those serving below him to do the same. This irked some of his superior officers, who believed things should always be done "by the book." During

World War II, however, Rickover's crafty maneuvers often helped ensure that the navy was ready to fight at peak efficiency.

Rickover's extensive electrical engineering background led to what would soon become his life's mission. After the war ended, he was assigned to represent the navy during work on the atomic bomb at Oak Ridge, Tennessee. Rickover immediately saw that nuclear power would be a revolutionary way to power ships and submarines. Nuclear power would allow submarines to remain at sea much longer and more safely than conventional diesel fuel. Many of Rickover's superior officers did not share his vision. They argued that such a change would be too expensive and take too much time. But Rickover would not take "no" for an answer and argued vehemently that if the U.S. Navy was to remain the best in the world there was no choice. More than once he pounded on tables and shouted at his startled and annoyed commanders. In the end, he won a job heading the new Naval Reactor Branch of the Atomic Energy Commission, which was designed to look into using nuclear power on ships and submarines.

Forty million dollars and seven years later, Rickover's first atomic submarine was launched in 1954. The *U.S.S. Nautilus* was only one of his many designs for such a craft. Soon he had completed plans for a massive aircraft carrier to be powered by a nuclear reactor. Again, the plans were stalled by opposition within the navy. Rickover complained loudly that the navy was making a stupid mistake in not going full speed ahead.

Such arrogance bothered many of his superiors, and Rickover was passed over twice for promotions. Technically, being ignored twice meant that Rickover was supposed to retire from the service. But Rickover refused to turn in his resignation, claiming he had been wronged by a few narrow-minded officers. A congressional investigation revealed several superior officers had in fact ignored Rickover for political and perhaps even anti-

Semitic reasons. Congress said there could be no arguing with Rickover's record of achievement, and he was promoted to rear admiral in 1953.

Rickover spent much of the rest of his career building a nuclear-powered fleet that was the most powerful in the world. But he also worried about the future of the United States. He, along with President Dwight Eisenhower, spoke out against the dangers of big industries becoming too closely tied to the military. The two believed such ties would lead to corruption and inefficiency caused by those hoping to make a profit selling arms to the military. They were proven correct, as what Eisenhower labeled "the military-industrial complex" caused government military spending to expand well into the 1980s, pushing the government into debt.

In 1982, Hyman Rickover used the occasion of his retirement to complain that the administration of President Ronald Reagan had wasted huge sums of tax dollars with an unprecedented military buildup. He also expressed deep regret at the role he played in the rise of nuclear weapons throughout the world, and he pleaded for an end to the arms race. During his last years, Rickover established a foundation to study and aid the educational process in the United States. Rickover died in Arlington, Virginia, at the age of 86.

Jascha Heifetz

VIOLINIST
1901–1987

Born in Vilna, Lithuania, Jascha Heifetz (YAH-shah HY-fits) first played a violin at the age of three. His father was his first music teacher. When he was six, Jascha had mastered Mendelssohn's violin concerto, an astounding achievement for a person of any age. One year later, Heifetz performed the piece in public for the first time. From his first recital, he had utter confidence in his own ability. He remembered looking at his father before he took the stage. "Pay no attention to the crowd," his father said. "Only play your best." When the young cellist who was accompanying him lost his way in the score, Jascha was not flustered and continued playing without a moment's hesitation. "Those were my first steps toward musical independence," he later remembered.

At nine years of age, he entered the St. Petersburg Conservatory, where his musical genius seemed to grow daily, astounding everyone but himself. In truth, although he was blessed with an almost supernatural ability, much of his brilliance was achieved through hard work. Until the end of his life, he would say there is only one way to be a great musician—practice.

At age ten, Heifetz toured Russia. A year later, he made his debut across Europe. In 1917, still only sixteen years old, he performed at Carnegie Hall. Even in New York, a city famous for having seen everything, a buzz of excitement surrounded the prodigy. Heifetz seemed unaffected by the acclaim, remaining a polite, quiet young man. He practiced hard every day, always believing he could improve some subtle aspect of his playing.

During the Russian Revolution of 1917, music was interrupted by historic events. Communists seized control, and the Heifetz family, not knowing what lay in store for wealthy Jews under this new regime, fled the country. They decided to make the long journey to America—first by traveling across Siberia to Japan, and then by ship to San Francisco.

Seemingly unaffected by such turmoil in his life, Heifetz continued to play brilliantly. He performed in London in 1920, Australia in 1921, across Asia in 1923, and in Palestine in 1926. By now, Heifetz was earning several thousand dollars for each concert, an unheard-of sum at the time. Critics ran out of adjectives to describe the perfect tone and musicality of his playing. All agreed he was among the very best ever to have put a bow to a violin.

Despite the accolades, Heifetz's life was not without controversy. In 1953, he decided to play a piece by the German composer Richard Strauss during a concert in Israel. Since the Holocaust in World War II, works by

German composers had not been played on Israeli soil. To Heifetz, however, the piece was only beautiful music having nothing to do with politics. He did not understand how strongly many Israelis felt about such things. Following the concert, Heifetz was attacked outside his hotel. A young Zionist swung an iron bar and struck him in the arm. No serious physical damage was done, but the incident made Heifetz a recluse. He ceased to play in public for as long as twenty months on several occasions.

Heifetz was always perfectly elegant, if a bit cold and distant. And he played his violin in concert the same way, standing stiffly on stage, his face expressionless. He wanted the audience to hear what he was playing, not watch him play it. "My art is the art of listening," he explained, "not the art of seeing." Today, hundreds of recordings allow new generations to listen to his genius.

Barney Ross

CHAMPION BOXER AND WAR HERO

1909–1967

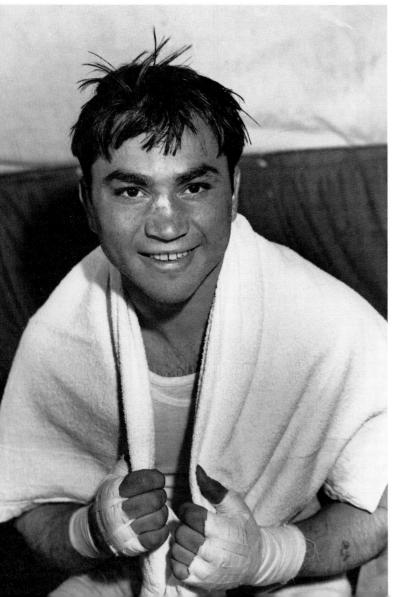

Barnet David Rasofsky's life was destined to be made into a movie—but he would be known to the world as Barney Ross. In 1924, his father, a grocer, was murdered during a robbery. Isadore Rasofsky, a scholar of the ancient Jewish text called the Talmud, had tried to pass his deep spirituality onto his son, but Barney had little interest in his Jewish heritage. After his father's death, Barney ran the grocery store and cared for his sickly mother. He was just fourteen years old. The family was so poor that Barney's two brothers and a sister were sent to an orphanage. His goal in life became to reunite his family.

In hopes of making money fast, Barney Ross became involved with organized crime in his neighborhood. He helped local criminals run an illegal gambling operation. But soon he discovered boxing. In 1926, he won the New York-Chicago Inter-City Golden Gloves featherweight championship. A year later, he became a professional boxer. When he won the lightweight title in 1933, he was able at last to reunite his family.

In 1934, Ross gained weight and strength and won the welterweight title but lost it in a rematch the same year. In 1938, he took a terrible beating at the hands of a challenger. Fans and sportswriters at ringside could not believe he remained standing for all fifteen rounds. He decided to retire from the ring and open a restaurant in Chicago. Also, he had just been married.

Ross decided he would settle down, run his business, and raise a family. Just when he thought his life would be uneventful, word began reaching the United States of Hitler's atrocities against the Jews of Europe. Though Ross had not been a practicing Jew since his father's death, the news made him angry, and he felt a sudden deep connection to his father. Ross decided to join the Marines and help fight the Nazis and Japanese. At first, Ross was rejected by the Marines because he was too old (at age thirty-two). But thanks to his fame as a boxer, he was soon admitted anyway. In 1942, he was sent to Guadalcanal, a small island in the Pacific Ocean occupied by Japanese troops. Ross was one of a group of reinforcements sent in to help Marines who had been fighting for many weeks to take the island. The battles had been terrible and bloody. Japanese troops had built strong fortifications and each foot of ground cost many men their lives.

When Ross's platoon landed on the beach, one of his group was immediately hit by a Japanese bullet. Ross and three others tried to drag the wounded man to safety, but suddenly a Japanese machine gunner opened fire, killing the wounded man and hitting everyone but Ross. When Ross jumped into a shell hole for cover, he found two more wounded Marines

After World War II, Ross was one of many prominent American Jews who rallied public support for the creation of Israel as a Jewish state.

there. For the next thirteen hours, Barney Ross defended his position single-handedly. He used all of his bullets, then the bullets of his fellow Marines. When he ran out of ammunition, Ross threw his remaining hand grenades at the Japanese positions all around him, fixed his bayonet to his rifle, and prepared to die.

During the night, he was hit with shrapnel in the leg, hand, and arm. He had also become dizzy with a case of malaria. Throughout this nightmare, he found himself praying in Hebrew as he had during his boyhood. Nearly delirious, Ross awaited the inevitable enemy attack that would end his life and the lives of his comrades. Miraculously, thanks to his tremendous determination and physical stamina, Ross survived the night and was rescued at daybreak by a new platoon. These rescuers found twenty-two dead enemy soldiers surrounding Ross's shell hole.

For his heroism, Ross was immediately promoted and awarded the Silver Star and Distinguished Service Cross. But the malaria he had contracted in the shell hole left him too weak to attend the awards ceremony. His wife took his place. Ross spent many months in military hospitals, where well-meaning doctors eased his pain with heavy doses of morphine. Soon, he became addicted to the drug.

During his battle with drug addiction and malaria, Ross found deep comfort in his renewed religious faith. After his recovery, he traveled the country telling others that with faith and inner strength they could overcome whatever difficulties life presented. Ross attributed his survival and triumph to what he called "a basic will to win," and wrote a book about his life called *No Man Stands Alone.* Friends knew Ross as a gentle and kind man even during his boxing days. He died a deeply religious man.

Benny Goodman

BAND LEADER
1909–1986

Benny Goodman was the eighth of eleven children. His father, a tailor, could hardly afford to feed his family. The Goodmans relied on the charity of their local Chicago synagogue to meet their basic needs. Fortunately, the synagogue offered classes in music. All the Goodman children attended. Instruments were handed out based on the child's size. Benny, small for his age, received a clarinet.

At age twelve, Benny began studying with the clarinet soloist of the Chicago Symphony Orchestra. By the time he was sixteen years old, Benny was an accomplished musician, worthy of notice by professionals. In the early 1930s, he traveled between New York and Los Angeles playing for various jazz bands and orchestras.

In 1933, Goodman met John Hammond, a wealthy music producer. Hammond recognized that Goodman had the potential to be a truly great musician and began guiding his development. Hammond teamed Goodman with various players he thought could stretch Goodman's abilities. Goodman recorded, played live shows, and performed on radio for a year, always honing his craft, but yearning to play something new and different. In 1934, Goodman formed his first permanent band and began working with arrangers Fletcher Henderson and Benny Carter to give a new shape to jazz music. He wanted a sound that was rich and symphonic, but that had "swing"—a beat that made you tap your feet.

The music they played was not all that was new about the Benny Goodman Orchestra. In the 1930s, African-Americans and Caucasians rarely mixed, and certainly never played in a band together. There were music clubs for "Negroes" and others for "whites only." Benny Goodman never considered a man's skin color when he chose his musicians. Such decisions were based solely on how well a musician played. Men like Teddy Wilson and Lionel Hampton, both black, could sure play. Lionel Hampton said years later: "The most important thing Benny Goodman did was to put Teddy Wilson and me in that band. It was instant integration."

It hardly crossed Goodman's mind that a fully integrated band was breaking new ground. But the Benny Goodman Orchestra was integrated ten years before the magnificent Jackie Robinson starred for baseball's Brooklyn Dodgers, and long before the U.S. Army saw fit to allow African-Americans to serve alongside whites.

During the winter of 1934–35, Benny Goodman's big band toured the country playing their newly invented "swing" music. The long trip proved to be a disappointing one. Audiences were unenthusiastic—and often outnumbered by band members. Many clubs at which the band was scheduled to appear canceled their shows. Goodman was heartbroken. By the time the group arrived at the Palomar Ballroom in Los Angeles, the band just wanted to go back to New York and start over again. Goodman later recalled, "I thought we'd finish the engagement in California and take the train back to New York and that would be it. I'd just be a clarinetist again."

Instead, the Benny Goodman Orchestra made musical history at the Palomar. When trumpeter Bunny Berigan lifted his horn to his lips and blew his raucous solo on "Sugar Foot Stomp," the crowd roared with delight. That roar, said Goodman years later, "was one of the sweetest sounds I ever heard in my life!" Soon, the audience stopped dancing and stood mesmerized by the thick, sweet sound of the horn section, the crazy rhythms of drummer Gene Krupa, and the melodic "swinging" sound of Goodman's clarinet. After each number they broke out in wild applause and whistling. From that day forward, the band was a hit, and Goodman quickly became known as "The King of Swing."

Following the band's brilliant night at the Palomar, they were signed to play for a coast-to-coast radio show called "Let's Dance." Soon, swing music was a national rage. Excited by swing's precision, drive, and musicianship, band leaders began completely rethinking their music.

The Benny Goodman band included many jazz greats through the years. Harry James, Lionel Hampton, Teddy Wilson, Gene Krupa, Dick Haymes, and singers Patti Page and Peggy Lee were among the best musicians in the country, and all broke through with the Goodman band. Even as swing caught on, Goodman was already working to push jazz even further. He formed a trio with drummer Gene Krupa and pianist Teddy Wilson. The three musicians experimented late into the night with new sounds. The group got even hotter when Goodman added vibraphonist Hampton to the mix. The work of these small bands would lead to artists like Charlie Parker, Dizzy Gillespie, and the so-called "bebop" jazz of the 1940s and 1950s.

In 1938, the Benny Goodman Orchestra played the first jazz concert in Carnegie Hall's history. Band members proudly wore white tie and tails for the occasion. A *New York Times* critic present that night wrote of Goodman's "quicksilver brilliance of improvisation, backed by more jazz technique than any other clarinetist can approach." This would not be the last time Goodman played in Carnegie Hall. He never lost his admiration for classical music and played several concerts with the New York Philharmonic. In 1940, he commissioned Bela Bartok to compose a piece for him and the Budapest String Quartet. The work, titled *Contrasts,* represented the newest ideas in classical music.

When Hollywood makes a movie of your life story there is no doubt you have hit it big. *The Benny Goodman Story* starred Steve Allen and was a big hit with audiences in 1955. The following year, Goodman took his band on a tour of the Far East, where his music was already enormously popular. They played sold-out shows in Hong Kong, Singapore, and Tokyo. In Russia, 200,000 people came to hear them. This tour was a lot more fun than their first one! Hits like "String of Pearls" and "Satin Doll" still sound great today and are played by jazz bands across the world.

When Benny Goodman died of a heart attack at the age of seventy-seven, the music world mourned. All the best musicians attended his funeral and expressed admiration and gratitude for his brilliant music, as well as his integrity and high moral standards. Goodman ought to be remembered as the man who integrated orchestras in the United States, as well as one of the greatest musicians America has ever produced.

Edwin Land

INVENTOR
1909–1991

When Edwin Land was a seventeen-year-old freshman at Harvard University, he took a walk one night and noticed the glare of the streetlights lining the main street in Cambridge, Massachusetts. It seemed to him that there might be great benefit in inventing a material that could filter out such harsh glare while allowing softer light of the moon to pass through. The problem stayed with him and kept him thinking. Such ponderings took up most of his time at school. Finally, he decided it was college that was getting in the way of his inventing, rather than the other way around.

So Land quit college at the age of twenty and began developing what he called a "polarizing filter" to eliminate glare. His father, a scrap-iron dealer who had never been able to attend college, was greatly disappointed by his son's decision. He argued vehemently that Edwin stay in school. But Edwin would not listen.

By the time Edwin Land was twenty-two years old, he had perfected a type of thin plastic for cameras and sunglasses that greatly reduced glare while not interfering with one's sight. In 1932, Land took the modest profits he made from sales of his "J Sheet" and co-founded Land-Wheelwright Laboratories in Cambridge. Five years later, he established the Polaroid Corporation to market products created in the Land-Wheelwright labs. By the late 1930s, Polaroid had become world famous for its amazing inventions—everything from instant X rays, to polarized lenses for sunglasses. Soon, the U.S. military put a number of Land's patents to work in World War II. Antiaircraft gunsights and night-vision goggles were fitted with Polaroid lenses. And when the U.S. Air Force built the U2 spy plane to fly more than 1 mile (1.6 kilometers) above Earth and take photographs of the ground below, the plane carried a camera and lenses designed and manufactured by Polaroid. These photographs were so sharp and clear that military experts could identify objects on the ground as small as a shoebox.

As years went by, much of the work at Land-Wheelwright Laboratories was devoted to discovering just how the eye and brain perceive images. To understand the incredibly complex system that allowed human beings to see became Land's consuming passion. One of his most important discoveries was that humans perceive color by comparing three or more different images using various parts of the eye and brain. This realization led, in 1941, to the invention of 3-D (three-dimensional) movies that could be viewed using Polaroid filtering glasses to "trick" the eye. During the 1940s and 1950s, such 3-D movies were extremely popular, and the technology is

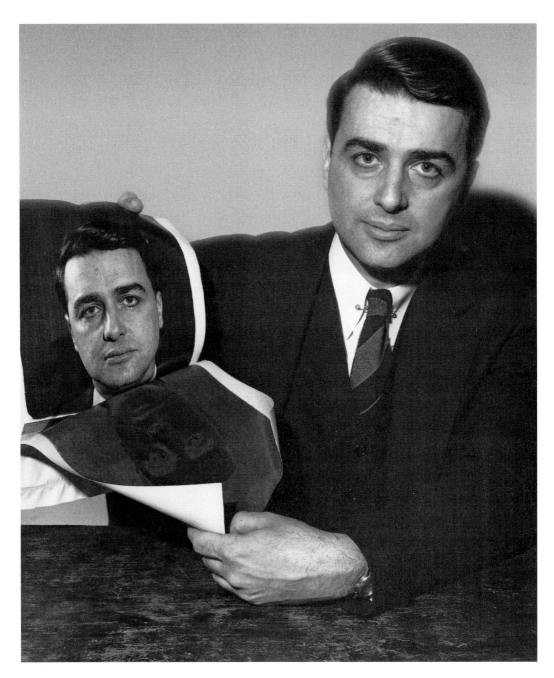

Edwin Land shows how easily a photograph can be made using "instant" photography.

still in use today. During this time, work began in earnest on the invention that would bring more fame than ever to Edwin Land and his Polaroid Corporation. American amateur photographers were accustomed to waiting a week or more to see prints of their snapshots. Land believed it was possible to develop photos instantly. Countless hours and various chemical processes and materials went into perfecting a manageable system of instant photography. In 1948, "taking a Polaroid" became all the rage, as families gathered around a snapshot and watched it develop in a mere two minutes. The drawback to these early Polaroids was that they came out of the camera wet, covered with a sheet of plastic that was later stripped off and discarded. By 1970, such inconveniences had been solved by Land-Wheelwright technicians. The SX70, a pocket-sized camera that delivered dry photos instantly, became one of the most popular cameras ever to hit the American market.

In all, Edwin Land secured more than 500 patents in plastics and light technology. Without having finished college himself, he became a professor first at Harvard University and later at the Massachusetts Institute of Technology (MIT). Though he earned more than half a billion dollars from his Polaroid Corporation, Land lived modestly until the end of his life, content to continue thinking, tinkering, and changing the way human beings see the world.

Jonas Salk

DEVELOPED POLIO VACCINE
1914–1995

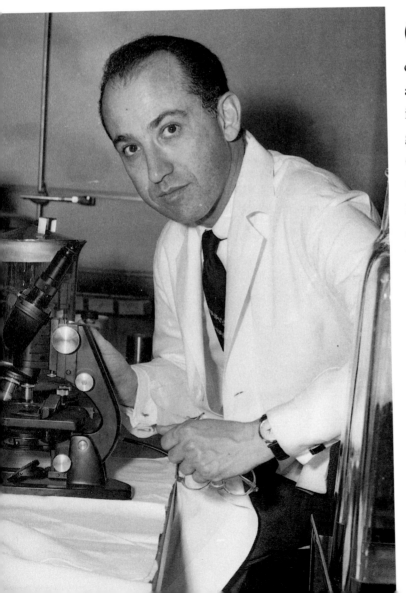

Great inventions and discoveries are almost never achieved in a single flash of inspiration. It is through dogged determination in the face of almost countless failures that most people find their way into the history books. Dr. Jonas Salk was one such iron-willed genius. In 1914, when Salk was born, polio was a dreaded disease, one of the great cripplers and killers. Tens of thousands of American citizens contracted the disease each year. Many died, and most survivors were unable to walk. Polio patients suffered painful paralysis of the limbs and deterioration of the muscles and nerves. The disease struck suddenly and without warning. Terrible fear entered any household when a child complained of a stiff neck or leg pain during the summer months. Rumors flew widely, and panic struck any neighborhood where a case of polio was reported.

When Salk was a child, it seemed impossible that he would grow up to find a vaccine that would virtually wipe polio from the face of the earth. Jonas was not much interested in science. He was a smart boy who loved baseball and much preferred reading comic books and novels to peering into a microscope. Still, Salk won nearly every academic honor it was possible to win and was admitted to the City College of New York when he was only fifteen years old.

Salk decided he would become a lawyer and took courses to prepare him for law school. Simply to broaden his background, he enrolled in several science courses as well. Soon he found himself fascinated by his biology course. He was so enthralled by the operations of the human body that he abandoned the law and entered New York University's Medical School. There, he embarked on research to develop a flu vaccine. The brilliant virologist Thomas Francis, Jr., headed the project and taught Salk a great deal about the nature of viruses.

It was during this time that Salk became obsessed with the notion of ending polio's reign of terror. In the summer, his own children were often afraid to go swimming because water carried the virus. This was how President Franklin D. Roosevelt contracted the disease as a young man. Polio had left Roosevelt unable to walk without the aid of leg braces.

At the University of Pittsburgh, Jonas Salk established a laboratory devoted solely to finding a vaccine against polio. His work was greatly assisted by that of Dr. John Enders, who won the 1954 Nobel Prize in medicine for discovering a means of growing the polio virus in large quantities for research purposes. Night and day, Salk worked at the problem of a vaccine. His colleagues were astounded by his determination to destroy the disease. He often spent twenty hours a day, seven days a week, in the laboratory. Trying one serum after another, Salk reasoned that if he simply kept working, kept pushing forward, one of his formulas would prove successful. Meanwhile, the enemy disease provided him with plenty of motive. During the American polio epidemic of 1952 alone, 57,626 people contracted the disease. Of those, more than 3,300 died. Many others lost the use of their legs and suffered terrible pain.

Salk's breakthrough finally came in 1953, when he created a "dead virus" serum. Injecting a vaccine that contained dead polio virus cells helped the body's immune system to create antibodies, which later helped fight off live virus cells. The serum appeared to work when tested in animals, but many people questioned the wisdom of injecting even dead polio virus into the human system. To prove his confidence in the new vaccine, Salk injected himself and his children over the objections of government doctors who urged a longer animal-testing period. Salk declared that there was no time to waste. Too many people had died and suffered already. For days, Salk and his family waited to see if he or his children contracted the disease from the serum. When they did not, many people volunteered for injections.

By 1954, the vaccine was accepted as effective. In 1957, Dr. Albert Sabin (also a Jewish American) perfected an oral vaccine that used live samples of the virus. The Sabin vaccine proved even more effective than Salk's vaccine.

To further efforts to prevent and cure human diseases, Salk founded the Salk Institute for Biological Studies in La Jolla, California. Today, the institute attracts the best researchers worldwide and provides them with state-of-the-art laboratories and generous funding. Until his death in 1995, Jonas Salk never stopped working to save humans from the suffering caused by viruses. Even in his late seventies, Salk worked long hours in hopes of creating a serum to stop the spread of AIDS. Many doubt there will ever be a true vaccine to fight AIDS, but Salk argued that it is only a matter of time and tireless work before this disease is stopped too.

Arthur Miller

Most famous as the author of *Death of a Salesman*, Arthur Miller has spent a lifetime in the theater. Miller ranks along with Tennessee Williams as the most celebrated American playwright in theater history.

Born in New York City's Harlem to working-class parents, Miller was raised as a Jew. Though he ceased to practice Jewish customs as an adult, he believed his "Jewishness" taught him lessons that are evident in his work: "There is tragedy in the world . . . but the world must continue . . . Jews can't afford to revel too much in the tragic because it might overwhelm them." Miller claims this "Jewish outlook" on life prevents him from writing plays that end in total despair and hopelessness.

As a young man, Miller had little interest in books or school, though he was an excellent high school football player and track athlete. Until he was seventeen years old, Miller read little besides comic books. But when he stumbled upon Fyodor Dostoyevsky's *The Brothers Karamazov,* Miller fell in love with words and writing. He was so deeply moved by the world Dostoyevsky created that he longed to create such works himself.

After his high school graduation in 1932, Miller decided he wanted to attend the University of Michigan and study playwrighting. Several obstacles stood in his way. His father, a clothing manufacturer whom Miller described as a "gruff entrepreneur" was not much excited by his son's likely unprofitable career choice. The family business had been badly damaged by the Great Depression. There was no money for college tuition, and Miller's poor high school grades eliminated any chance of a scholarship. But Miller would not be stopped in his quest to become a playwright. During the next two years, he read all of Shakespeare's plays and worked at various jobs to earn his college tuition. He worked briefly for his father and hated the business. He could not stand the abuse his father—and his father's salesmen—had to take from buyers. These experiences in sales would later influence his writing.

Following graduation from the University of Michigan in 1938, Miller went to work for the Federal Theater Project. This was a government program designed to help artists struggling to survive the tough economic times. Miller taught writing for the project. He also began writing radio plays for NBC and CBS. In 1944, a producer finally staged Miller's first play, *The Man Who Had All the Luck.* It was a complete failure. Miller even went so far as to eliminate the script from later collections of his work. The play was confusing to audiences and presented its political themes in such a way that theatergoers lost interest. Miller learned from his mistakes, and his 1947 play *All My Sons* was a huge success. Audiences cared about the characters in the play and reviewers praised the realistic dialogue. *All My Sons* went on to win the prestigious New York Drama Critic's Circle Award for 1947.

"I couldn't see myself going on writing play after play and getting absolutely nowhere," Miller said later. "I sat down . . . to write a play about which nobody could say to me, as they had with all the other plays, 'What does this mean?' or 'I don't understand that.'" Miller labored two years over *All My Sons* and clearly learned a great deal from the process. His next play took him just six weeks to write and changed theater history. *Death of a Salesman* won every major award for drama in 1949 including the Pulitzer Prize, the Tony Award, and the New York Drama Critic's Circle Award. It ran on Broadway for 742 performances.

The *New York Times* drama critic said of the play: "Arthur Miller has written a superb drama. From every point of view, *Death of a Salesman* is rich and memorable. . . . Mr. Miller has looked with compassion into the hearts of some ordinary Americans and quietly transferred their hope and anguish to the theater." The play's protagonist, Willy Loman, is an aging traveling salesman. Loman, who has spent his life in the business of selling products through his personal charm and ended up with little to show for it, has reached a low point. No longer young, out of energy and jokes, Loman realizes he had "the wrong dreams. All, all wrong." Only his loving wife and sons save his life from being meaningless. Proof that the play's characters and feelings are universal can be found in its success in Beijing, China, in 1983. It remains one of only a few Western plays ever seen by Chinese audiences.

The 1950s were a strange time in the United States. Fear that the Soviet Union would attempt a Communist takeover of the country resulted in the rise to prominence of Senator Joseph McCarthy. McCarthy held a series of hearings designed to root out Communists hiding in the government and various industries. As a result, many people were called to testify before

McCarthy's committee and were expected to name anyone they knew who had any connection to Communist activities in the United States. It was not uncommon for artistic people to be interested in Communist causes—workers' rights, social justice, and equality for African-Americans and women. As a result, many individuals connected with the entertainment industry were called to testify. When Miller's turn came, he refused to cooperate in any way. Miller's refusal led to his being indicted on charges of obstruction of justice. These charges were later dropped.

The experience led to what many believe is Miller's most powerful and brilliant work, *The Crucible,* written in 1953. On the surface, the play is about the Salem witch trials of the 1700s. In Salem, Massachusetts, popular fears that witches were endangering the town led to the "trial" and subsequent execution of several women. Miller used this spectacle to mimic Joseph McCarthy's modern-day Communist chase, which Miller had labeled a "witch-hunt."

From 1965 to 1969, Miller served as president of Poets, Playwrights, Editors, Essayists, and Novelists (PEN), the international writers' association. In 1973, he became Professor of Drama at the University of Michigan. In 1981, his television screenplay *Playing for Time,* about Jewish musicians in a German concentration camp, won a Peabody Award. He branched out into autobiography with his book *Timebends* in 1987. Miller remained a presence on Broadway with his play *The Last Yankee* in 1993 and *Broken Glass* in 1994. He even assisted Hollywood filmmakers in adapting *The Crucible* into a film that was released in 1996.

A *Paris Review* interviewer once described Arthur Miller as "a storyteller, a man with a marvelous memory, a simple man with a capacity for wonder, concerned with people and ideas." Others have said that he is like an eagle, alert, intense, and watchful. Arthur Miller is a man of deep integrity who believes in the power of art: "The creative spirit . . . is holy, and it takes great effort, a kind of prayer, to keep it alive and to nurture it."

Julius and Ethel Rosenberg

CONVICTED AS SPIES
Julius (1918–1953)   Ethel (1915–1953)

Ethel and Julius Rosenberg were both born on the Lower East Side of New York City. Among the first generation of children born to European Jewish immigrants, they both attended the Downtown Talmud Torah synagogue. The two met at local Communist Party meetings, fell in love, and married. Their connection to the Communist Party seemed the only thing even slightly out of the ordinary about the Rosenbergs, but it led to their infamous place in American history.

Ethel Greenglass graduated from high school when she was sixteen years old and became a secretary to help support her family. Julius Rosenberg came from a religious family that urged him to study Jewish texts and become a rabbi. But Julius was more interested in politics than religion. While at the City College of New York working toward a degree in electrical engineering, he became involved with the Young Communist League. It was here he met Ethel Greenglass. They believed in workers' rights and wanted to help the poor. They were married soon after his college graduation.

Julius got a job working for the U.S. Army Signal Corps. He became an engineer inspector in 1942, soon after the United States entered World War II. During the war, the Soviet Union was an American ally. But after the war, the Soviet Union's Communist system was seen as a threat to the American way of life, and the two countries became enemies. Although he and Ethel quit the Communist Party in 1945, Julius was immediately fired by the army when his superior officers learned he had once been chairman of the Communist Party's local branch.

Julius then worked briefly for the Emerson Radio Corporation, but he quit when Ethel's brother offered him a business opportunity. David Greenglass was starting up a machine shop, and Julius jumped at the chance to be a partner in the new business. Unfortunately, the business failed, and Julius and Ethel struggled for enough money to feed their two sons.

It is unclear exactly what happened to the Rosenbergs in 1949 and 1950. David Greenglass had worked at Los Alamos during the military's top-secret refinement of the atomic bomb. When Greenglass was arrested for selling nuclear secrets to the Soviet Union in 1950, he confessed and claimed that Julius had been his partner in the spying operation. Julius denied any involvement. Arrested and jailed, Julius refused to cooperate with the Federal Bureau of Investigation (FBI). Soon, Ethel was also arrested. FBI files show that Ethel's arrest was calculated to make Julius Rosenberg confess. The agency had no reason to believe she had been involved in spying. Officially charged with conspiracy to commit espionage, both maintained their silence.

The most intricate workings of the law played an important role in the Rosenbergs' case. The fact that they were charged with *conspiracy* to commit espionage meant that prosecutors only had to prove that they had *planned* to be spies. The prosecution was not forced to prove that the conspiracy actually worked. Legal experts were not surprised when the Rosenbergs were found guilty of conspiracy to commit espionage. But when Judge Irving Kaufman ordered them put to death, most were shocked. Had the Rosenbergs been convicted of treason, rather than conspiracy, the death penalty would have been standard procedure. But never before had anyone convicted merely of conspiracy received a death sentence. Kaufman (also a Jewish American) stated that "atom spies" were a distinct threat to American security and that special severity was in order. Defense attorney Emanuel Bloch immediately appealed the case.

In 1952, Bloch's appeal failed. Again, the intricacies of the law had hurt the Rosenberg's case. Since the court had upheld the Rosenbergs' original conviction, it had no authority to change the Rosenbergs' sentence. But this was not the end of the Rosenberg case. A political magazine called *The National Guardian* ran a series of articles declaring the Rosenbergs were victims of what it called "American fascism." It claimed the United States had become so obsessed with destroying Communism that the country was losing sight of the justice and liberty guaranteed in the Constitution. After the U.S. Supreme Court refused to lighten the Rosenbergs' sentence, a public campaign was launched to bring about a stay of execution.

In October 1952, the Rosenbergs published a book. *The Death House Letters* contained the notes the two exchanged while confined in their cells

With the country furious with fear over Communism, many Americans openly rejoiced when the Rosenbergs were executed.

at Sing Sing prison. The letters talked of their fears and their longing to be reunited with each other and their children. The book brought an international response, and countless groups and individuals called for a reduction in the severity of their sentence. Twenty thousand letters and telegrams arrived at the White House each week asking President Harry Truman to help the Rosenbergs. Lawyers attempted any number of arguments to persuade the president to grant leniency, or to release the Rosenbergs altogether. Truman refused.

The original sentence called for the Rosenbergs to be executed on a Friday evening in June 1953. So as not to desecrate the Jewish Sabbath, authorities agreed to push up the execution so that it would take place before sundown. FBI files later revealed that agents still held out hope that the Rosenbergs would confess to spying and thus stop the execution. They did not confess. First Julius and then Ethel were strapped into the electric chair and put to death.

To this day, arguments over the Rosenberg case continue. The Rosenbergs denied ever having sold secrets to the Soviet Union. They claimed they had been framed by David Greenglass and a government looking for scapegoats after the Soviets built their own atomic bomb. Whatever the case, the execution of the Rosenbergs remains one of the most dramatic and darkest moments in American legal history.

Arnold "Red" Auerbach

BASKETBALL COACH AND EXECUTIVE
1917–

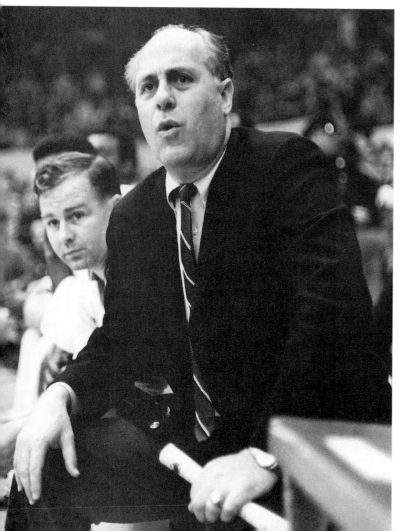

Red Auerbach helped to invent modern professional basketball. His policies as coach and later vice president and general manager of the Boston Celtics ushered in an intelligent, more athletic style of play and, more importantly, a new era of racial equality in the sport.

Auerbach got his start in pro basketball in 1946, when he had just been discharged from the navy. Auerbach convinced the owner of the Washington Capitols to let him coach the team. Auerbach helped break basketball's color line in 1950. Until that time an unwritten, so-called gentlemen's agreement had excluded blacks from the league. Auerbach and New York Knickerbocker coach Joe Lapchick agreed that each would allow an African-American player to join his team. The experiment proved successful, and nearly every team soon added blacks to their rosters.

Auerbach became coach of the Boston Celtics in 1950. Before his arrival, the Celtic franchise was nothing special. Four years later, Auerbach became the first coach to start five African-American players. Through another unspoken agreement, coaches previously had refused to do so. Many believed white fans would not pay to see an all-black team. When Auerbach's star forward Tommy Heinsohn, a white player, hurt his foot, Auerbach simply played his best substitute. Auerbach denied any heroics—Willie Nauls just happened to be black. The team won its next sixteen games with no drop in attendance.

In his fifteen-year reign as the Celtics' coach, Auerbach's teams were nearly unbeatable. He won his first world championship in the 1956–57 season, then won eight in a row from 1959 to 1966. The Celtics were a dynasty that has never been equaled in American sports history. Naturally, it was not only Auerbach's coaching that lifted the team. Having Hall of Famers Bill Russell, Bob Cousy, and Tommy Heinsohn on the squad did not hurt. Near the end of each winning game, with the Celtics holding an insurmountable lead, Auerbach would lean back in his chair and announce the contest was over by lighting up his famous victory cigar. The fans at the Boston Garden always erupted with delight.

Following the Celtics' championship in 1966, Auerbach decided to step down as coach. Still only 48 years old, he retired as the National Basketball Association's (NBA) all-time winningest coach. But Auerbach did not leave the game, or the Celtics. He became the team's vice president and general manager, which meant that his first job was to choose his own successor as coach. Without hesitation, he hired his star center, Bill Russell, making him the first African-American to coach a major professional sports team in the United States. As general manager, Auerbach helped assemble the great Larry Bird-led Celtics teams of the 1980s. In all, Auerbach has enjoyed sixteen world championships as an employee of the Boston Celtics.

In 1968, the Basketball Hall of Fame in Springfield, Massachusetts, named Red Auerbach Greatest Coach in the History of the NBA. Auerbach has received seven honorary degrees from various colleges and universities. He has written five books on basketball, some of which rank among the most popular on the sport.

In 1985, Auerbach established the Red Auerbach Fund to promote youth recreation and development programs in Boston. Also, his Red Auerbach Youth Foundation sponsors an annual Celtics basketball clinic for Boston's inner city youth, as well as granting eight college scholarships yearly to athletes who demonstrate superior leadership in their communities. Like Branch Rickey, the Brooklyn Dodgers' executive who put Jackie Robinson in a major league uniform, Red Auerbach was strong enough to do what was right despite pressure to maintain the status quo. He remains active within the Celtics organization, though he is no longer allowed by law to light up a victory cigar in the Boston Garden.

Jewish Americans and the Civil Rights Movement

In 1896, the United States Supreme Court decided that separation of the races was permissible so long as the facilities provided for blacks were equal to those provided for whites—which they never were. By 1910, African-Americans had been systematically stripped of the ability to vote in most southern states, and the governor of Mississippi vowed to defend such policies by saying, "If it is necessary, every Negro in the state will be lynched; it will be done to maintain white supremacy." Between 1889 and 1918, it is estimated that 3,224 black men and women were murdered in this way throughout the country.

During these years, life was also difficult for Jewish Americans, though they suffered few violent attacks. The Ku Klux Klan declared Jews enemies of the United States, and various newspapers, including automobile mogul Henry Ford's *Dearborn Independent,* were devoted to attacking Jews and other minorities. Even in the respectable press, Jews were sometimes caricatured as big-nosed, dirty, and greedy. Father Coughlin, a committed anti-Semite, became a popular voice on radio during the 1930s. Universities created formal and informal quotas restricting the number of Jews admitted each year, and so-called "glass ceilings" denied Jews promotion to positions of power in various industries.

A shared struggle to overcome prejudice helped bring Jews and blacks together. In 1915, Leo Frank, a young Jewish manufacturer was falsely convicted of murdering a gentile girl. In an ensuing riot, Frank was lynched by a bloodthirsty mob. This murderous show of hatred frightened American Jews. Jewish community leaders now began to identify their own struggles more closely with those of African-Americans. And many African-Americans raised as Christians identified with the history of the Jews, who had suffered under slavery in ancient Egypt.

Jewish philanthropists like Herbert Lehman and Julius Rosenwald helped build the National Association for the Advancement of Colored People (NAACP) in 1909. Jewish-American Joel Spingarn, an early chairman of the organization, helped chart the direction of the civil rights movement from 1911 until his death in 1939. W. E. B. DuBois, the legendary African-American social scientist, dedicated his autobiography to Spingarn.

Julius Rosenwald was also instrumental in the rise of the Tuskegee Institute, which trained many talented African-Americans who would later contribute to the civil rights movement. Other powerful Jews became involved in the cause. When Mordecai Johnson, the president of Howard University, decided to set up a law school to train black attorneys, he asked Supreme Court Justice Louis Brandeis for advice. Eventually, Howard's excellent law school provided well-trained black attorneys who helped tear down fifty years of racist legislation. The law school's first president, Charles Houston, had worked closely with Felix Frankfurter, another Jewish-American Supreme Court justice.

Along with W. E. B. Dubois, Franz Boas, a Jew, worked to combat the idea that blacks were genetically inferior to whites. These two early social scientists convinced many people that any seeming inferiority among blacks was caused by the harsh conditions under which most were born and raised. Rabbis Stephen S. Wise and Emil Hirsch and social workers Lillian Wald and Henry Moskowitz were among the American Jews who stepped forward to help in the early days of the struggle to end injustices suffered by African-Americans.

During the 1940s, a number of organizations run by Jews fought for social justice. Many Jewish-controlled unions argued that the plight of blacks ought to be viewed as a problem for all human beings. Also, the American Jewish Congress launched a major campaign to break down discriminatory laws. Civil rights lawyers within the organization fought for fair educational opportunities and fair housing and employment. The Jewish Anti-Defamation League (ADL) helped see to it that laws were passed which hampered racist and terrorist activities of the Ku Klux Klan. Lawyers from the ADL won passage of legislation making it illegal to wear hoods and burn crosses without applying for permission in many states and cities. Stripped of their anonymity, the Klansmen lost much of their power.

In 1950, the American Jewish Congress funded an extensive study of the effect of school segregation on African-American children. The report helped lead to the famous 1954 Supreme Court case of *Brown vs. the Board of Education of Topeka, Kansas.* The decision in favor of Brown struck down the "separate but equal" ruling of 1896. The court ruled that the "hearts and minds" of black children suffered under conditions of segregation.

In 1955, Rosa Parks started the Montgomery bus boycott, and Martin Luther King, Jr., became the leader of the civil rights struggle. From then on, Jews served more in the background as African-Americans stepped forward in leadership roles. In the summer of 1961, King's Freedom Riders

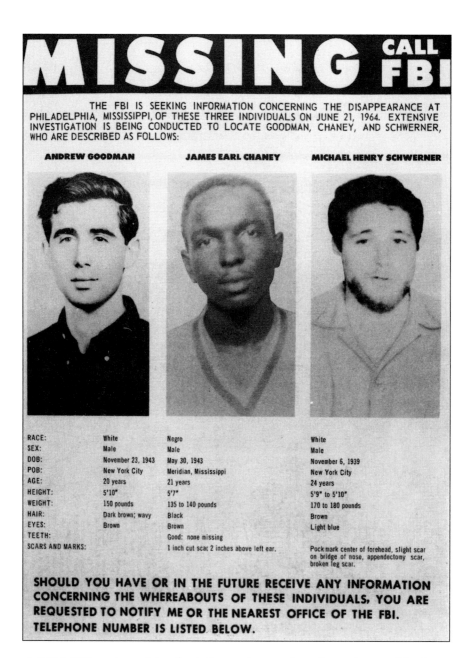

A 1964 FBI poster asking for information on the whereabouts of Andrew Goodman, James Chaney, and Michael Schwerner. The three young civil rights workers were later found murdered.

worked to desegregate bus transportation in the South. Of the whites on the trip, two-thirds were Jews. In 1964, the Student Non-violent Coordinating Committee organized "Freedom Summer" in Mississippi. Volunteers registered blacks to vote. At least one-third of these volunteers were Jewish Americans. Tragically, two of these young Jewish volunteers, Andrew Goodman and Michael Schwerner, were murdered along with James Chaney, a black student. Their murders shocked the nation and became one of the most important—yet tragic—moments in the civil rights movement.

In a 1965 interview, Dr. Martin Luther King, Jr., discussed the role of Jewish Americans in the fight for social justice: "How could there be anti-Semitism among Negroes when our Jewish friends have demonstrated their commitment to the principle of tolerance and brotherhood not only in the form of sizable contributions, but in many other tangible ways, and often at great personal sacrifice. . . . It would be impossible to record the contribution that the Jewish people have made towards the Negro's struggle for freedom—it has been so great."

From the 1970s to the present, the relationship between Jews and African-Americans has often been strained, many times violently opposed. Many factors contributed to such difficulties. As prejudice against Jews retreated, they moved into the mainstream of American society. At the same time, many black civil rights groups became more radical, advocated violence, or simply spoke against whites in general. Some prominent African-Americans supported Palestinian rights and opposed Israel on important issues. At the same time, Jewish leaders sometimes opposed affirmative- action legislation and community control of schools in low-income areas. Both stands caused resentment among blacks. Recently, Jesse Jackson and Louis Farrakhan, two important black leaders, have reportedly made anti-Semitic remarks. In 1991, violence and riots erupted in the Crown Heights area of Brooklyn when the car of an Orthodox Jew struck a black child.

Despite such problems, a long tradition of Jewish and African-American cooperation in the fight for equality has led to a solid foundation upon which to build relations. In a 1984 speech to the American Jewish Committee, African-American leader Vernon Jordan explained why blacks and Jews would always be united: "The reason is we need each other. We are both minorities in a society that has the capacity to frustrate our aspirations for full and unconditional equality. . . . Jews have an abiding interest in the preservation of civil rights. They have been denied those rights in the past. And they have an overriding interest in justice for all minorities, for they are themselves among the smallest of America's minority groups, hence, among the most vulnerable."

Leonard Bernstein

CONDUCTOR AND COMPOSER
1918–1990

Leonard Bernstein was a conductor, composer, pianist, author, educator, television star, Zionist, political activist, scholar, and producer. For many people throughout the world, Bernstein came to be classical music's ultimate representative, a kind of king. For Bernstein, his fame was always less important than his music. "Music is something terribly special," he once said. "It doesn't have to pass through the censor of the brain before it can reach the heart."

Leonard Bernstein was born in Lawrence, Massachusetts, to Ukrainian immigrant parents.

His father, Samuel, ran a beauty-supply store and hoped that Leonard would take over the business one day. When Leonard was ten, Samuel Bernstein agreed to store an old piano for a few months. Bernstein's parents, who had little interest in music, were surprised when their son fell in love with the instrument. He began taking lessons and soon proclaimed he would make music his life's work. Hearing this, Bernstein's father refused to pay for any more lessons. He never approved of his son's chosen career.

After getting his undergraduate degree at Harvard University, Bernstein attended the Curtis Institute of Music in Philadelphia. There he studied under Fritz Reiner, the great conductor of the Chicago Symphony Orchestra. In 1940, he worked with Boston Symphony Orchestra conductor Serge Koussevitzky, who became Bernstein's mentor. Reiner and Koussevitzky had very different styles. Reiner was a rigorous musician concerned with perfection of technique. Koussevitzky, on the other hand, was known for his passion and fire. The origin of Bernstein's greatness as a musician and composer may have been in his ability to bring together the best qualities of these two masters.

In 1940, having spent a year working with Koussevitzky, Bernstein took a twenty-five-dollar-a-week position with a music publisher. His job was to listen to recordings of jazz improvisations and transcribe the notes onto sheet music. He also wrote his own arrangements of current popular songs under the name Lenny Amber. Just as Bernstein integrated the techniques of his two great teachers, he would later bring together his knowledge of popular and classical forms of music.

Bernstein's big break came in 1943. Still only twenty-five years old, Bernstein was working as an assistant conductor of the New York Philharmonic. One night, Bernstein was forced to take the podium in place of a guest conductor who was ill. With almost no rehearsal time, Bernstein took charge of perhaps the most famous orchestra in the world and led them masterfully through a complex and difficult program. At its completion, the audience exploded into a tremendous ovation. Overnight, Leonard Bernstein became a star.

Bernstein would go on to become the first American-born musician to become a world-class conductor. Classical music was never the same following Bernstein's sudden rise. He was young and handsome. Wherever he went, teenage girls awaited him screaming, wanting only to touch him. Following each performance, security guards had to hustle him into a waiting limousine to escape the throngs of worshiping girls. Despite such distractions, Bernstein concentrated on his music and expanded his talents. During World War II, he began to compose works for symphony orchestra. He wrote the *Jeremiah Symphony* which won the 1943–44 New York City Music Critics' Circle award as the best new orchestral work of the season. In the same year, Bernstein composed music for a ballet called *Fancy Free.* Later the music was adapted for the Broadway stage as the hit musical *On the Town.*

During the late 1940s and 1950s, Bernstein taught at Brandeis University and guest-conducted in New York, Milan, and Tel Aviv. Always eager for a new way to experience and think about music, Bernstein accepted an offer to compose a musical score for the now-classic film *On the Waterfront.* The film is a powerful drama starring Marlon Brando, and Bernstein's score is very much part of the film's strength. Soon afterward, Bernstein's first attempt at writing a Broadway musical was a flop, although *Candide* is considered a classic today.

Candide's commercial failure did not discourage Bernstein. He loved Broadway and longed to write a great show for the stage. In the mid-1950s, he worked with choreographer Jerome Robbins, a young lyricist named Stephen Sondheim, and director Arthur Laurents on a musical, modern-day adaptation of Shakespeare's *Romeo and Juliet.* The musical was to be set in New York's Hell's Kitchen, a tough neighborhood of mostly Latino immigrants. The result of the collaboration is *West Side Story,* one of the greatest shows ever produced on Broadway (which was later turned into an equally successful film). At the age of thirty-nine, Bernstein stood at the center of both classical and popular music.

In 1958, Bernstein became musical director of the New York Philharmonic, a position of great power in the music world. He helped make famous the work of American composer Charles Ives, and he aggressively exposed American audiences to the brilliant symphonies of Gustav Mahler. Also, he began a campaign to teach children to love the music that so moved him. He began a series of "Young People's Concerts" for television. An entire generation of American children learned about music by listening to Bernstein explain the work he was about to conduct. It was on this series that Bernstein's personal charm made him world famous not only as a musician, but as a teacher. Writer Victor Navasky described the effect the show had on his generation as children: "He lured us onto the stage with him, and instantly it was as if we were in his living room and he was patting the piano bench saying 'Come on, sit down next to me, and I'll show you something incredible.' And he did. . . holding us with his every word until, miraculously, we actually began to understand how music worked and what made it so beautiful." Throughout his life, Bernstein worked to bring music to everyone, whether rich or poor, educated or uneducated, adult or child.

The passion Bernstein brought to music was legendary. Bernstein threw his whole body and soul into the work of bringing music to life from simple notes on a page. "My greatest performances come when I don't remember who I am, or where I am," he once said. A few critics thought Bernstein's "showmanship" detracted from the music, but conductor Herbert Blondsted felt such complaints were foolish: "He doesn't try to be that way. He is that way. He's completely himself when he makes music."

Once, composer Igor Stravinsky sat in the audience as Bernstein conducted his *Symphony of Psalms.* Afterward, when asked what he thought of Bernstein's interpretation of his composition, Stravinsky could say only, "Wow!" The result of such unrelenting success was that Bernstein gained more and more influence in the world of music, and the world in general. The "Omnibus Concerts," seen on public television, made him a star recognized even by those who cared nothing about classical music. Such notoriety made him influential in swaying public opinion and Bernstein began to use this power to advance causes he thought were important. He began hiring more African-Americans, Hispanics, Asians, and women as New York Philharmonic musicians. His activities at times proved controversial. There was much backlash in the 1960s when he sponsored a dinner on behalf of the Black Panthers, a politically radical and sometimes violent organization dedicated to advancing the cause of African-Americans.

Bernstein always had an idea of his place in history and relentlessly promoted his own career. During the 1967 Arab and Israeli War, Bernstein flew to Jerusalem and conducted a concert. A film crew followed his every move, and a documentary of the trip was released. The film helped the United States public better understand the war and won sympathy for Israel's cause. Twenty-one years later, Bernstein returned to Jerusalem to conduct an outdoor concert of Mahler's *Resurrection Symphony* to mark Israel's fortieth anniversary.

During the 1980s, when the world became aware of a disease called AIDS, Bernstein was one of the first celebrities to help fight it. In 1989, Bernstein became part of history yet again by conducting Beethoven's *Ninth Symphony* when the Berlin Wall was destroyed, signaling the end of Communist rule in East Germany and the reunification of the country. The symphony, also called the *Ode to Joy,* involves a huge chorus singing in German. For that occasion, Bernstein changed the word "joy," which is

In his later years, Leonard Bernstein achieved recognition as the greatest American composer and conductor of his time.

freude in German, to *freiheit,* which means "freedom." It was a stirring moment seen all over the world: Bernstein's white hair flying, his face contorted with effort, as he drove the orchestra ahead and the hundreds of voices rang out in celebration.

In 1985, Bernstein received a Lifetime Achievement Grammy Award. At a concert honoring his seventieth birthday, Bernstein said, "I have no further requests of the fates . . . except for [more] time. I've achieved more than I had any right to expect. Nobody has been as lucky as I have." Unfortunately, he did not receive much more time. Bernstein died at age 72 from heart failure brought on by a lifetime of heavy smoking. He was by far the most important among the many Jewish Americans who helped build American orchestras into world-class organizations (Fritz Reiner, Bruno Walter, and Serge Koussevitzky were all Jewish Americans).

Today, Bernstein remains a giant, the kind of artist against whom all others are measured. *Newsweek* magazine declared him "the greatest figure in the history of American music."

Betty Friedan

WOMEN'S RIGHTS ADVOCATE
1921–

During the 1960s and 1970s, a generation of American women refused to accept a secondary role in shaping their own destinies. Moving ahead from having won the right to vote in 1920, the women's movement next challenged the long-held idea that "a woman's place is in the home." An author, psychologist, professor, co-founder of the National Organization for Women, journalist, mother, and grandmother, Betty Friedan was perhaps the most influential leader of these women who changed the world.

She was born Betty Naomi Goldstein in Peoria, Illinois.

Her father was a jeweler, and her mother was a former newspaper reporter who gave up her job to raise a family. Friedan's mother regretted this decision. She encouraged her daughter to become a journalist and to value her career. Friedan attended Smith College in Massachusetts, the finest women's college in the United States, and graduated cum laude in 1942. During the 1940s, what would soon blossom into a new women's movement was just beginning. It was a revolution that started in living rooms across the United States. Women met in small groups for so-called "consciousness raising" sessions where each discussed her hopes, dreams, and frustrations in the context of being a woman in American society. Here, many women discovered that they shared with their neighbors and friends a desire for something more in their lives than a husband and children.

After her college graduation, Friedan decided to become a clinical psychologist and accepted a fellowship to study at the University of California at Berkeley. She might have gone on to become simply a very good clinical psychologist had she not soon married Carl Friedan. Carl Friedan started an advertising agency and moved his wife and three children to the California suburbs. Betty Friedan stayed home to raise her kids, keep the house, and work as a freelance writer. Though she loved her family, she found she was unfulfilled in this life.

Friedan began to wonder if other women felt trapped in their own homes. In 1957, fifteen years after her college graduation, Friedan wrote a questionnaire and mailed it to members of her graduating class at Smith College. Two hundred of her classmates responded in detail to her questions. Most were dissatisfied with their lives. They described the pain of trying to conform to society's picture of women as perfect wives and mothers. A clear pattern of frustration, sadness, and guilt could be traced to the fact that while women were admired in these roles, they were not allowed to be or do much of anything else.

Clearly, this was a profound discovery. How many millions of women, Friedan wondered, suffered in silence? In 1963, Friedan published a book called *The Feminine Mystique,* which helped to answer that question. Three million copies were sold, and a revolution began among American housewives.

The Feminine Mystique begins with a description of a problem: " . . . the problem that has no name. . . . The problem lay buried, unspoken, for many years in the minds of American women. . . . Each suburban wife struggled with it alone. As she made the beds, shopped for groceries, matched slipcover material . . . she was afraid to ask even of herself the silent question— 'Is this all?'" Friedan argued that women ought to be allowed to pursue their dreams. Cooking and cleaning, she said, was not enough to fulfill most women.

Today, such ideas are commonplace. But before Friedan's book, they were rarely talked about. Friedan portrayed the average housewife as the victim of a system that discriminated against her, and she argued forcefully that a woman's identity could not be found in the sort of furniture she chose for her home, or the good behavior and success of her children. Women needed accomplishments of their own.

In 1966, Friedan helped found the National Organization for Women (NOW). NOW's goal was to bring women into political power. As NOW's president through 1970, Friedan rose to even more national prominence as a debater, lecturer, and protester for women's rights.

But during the women's movement that she helped launch, and to the present day, Betty Friedan has argued for more than just women's rights. She has fought tirelessly for a full range of *human* rights. Friedan's book *The Fountain of Age* argued on behalf of older citizens undervalued and ignored by an American population obsessed with youth and physical beauty. In her book *The Second Stage,* Friedan wrote that the women's movement had to enter a new phase. She called for a shift in focus to address the needs of families. During the 1980s, Friedan spoke out about men who worked too hard and were never allowed a chance to enjoy time with their families. Fathers, argued Friedan, must become full and equal partners in the raising of children and keeping the home. She caused controversy at West Point when she worked to help women integrate into the military. Many feminists felt that the movement ought to stand in opposition to military spending and war rather than insisting on jobs as soldiers, but Friedan saw this controversial move into soldiering as part of the developing "personhood of women."

Ultimately, Friedan's message has always been that people ought to be involved in caring. Everyone ought to care about themselves and the world, and they should fight for social justice. Today, many of Friedan's revolutionary ideas are widely accepted. Women routinely work outside the home and occupy positions of authority that would have been unheard of just thirty years ago. *The Feminine Mystique* might be seen as a sort of Declaration of Independence. Friedan's book sparked women around the world to protest the unjust restrictions placed upon them by society.

Henry Kissinger

SECRETARY OF STATE

1923–

During the 1970s, Henry Kissinger became one of the most powerful men in the world. As the U.S. secretary of state under Richard Nixon and Gerald Ford, he presided over the war in Vietnam, the beginnings of American diplomacy in China, and the peak of the long Cold War with the Soviet Union. In every case, Kissinger helped to decide the course of history. He remains a controversial figure. Some historians believe he was a genius who helped the United States through a difficult time; others believe Kissinger's policies and personality caused problems the United States might have otherwise avoided.

Kissinger was born Heinz Alfred Kissinger in Furth, Germany. His father was a teacher in Furth until Adolf Hitler came to power and banned all Jews from the profession. In 1938, seeing that Hitler was only growing stronger and more dangerous, the Kissingers fled to England and soon emigrated to the United States. Perhaps this betrayal of his family by the German government made a strong impression on young Heinz. Throughout his career in government, he was very secretive and distrusted many of the officials with whom he worked.

After arriving in the United States, the teenage Kissinger quit high school and took a job in a factory to help his family earn some money. Later, he joined the army and was part of army intelligence in Germany during World War II. After the war, the GI Bill allowed Kissinger to go to college. Kissinger was accepted into Harvard University and began his studies in 1947. History fascinated Kissinger. He happily stayed up all night devouring book after book. He graduated summa cum laude and Phi Beta Kappa, the highest honors a student can achieve, and accomplished this in just three years! His senior thesis on the meaning of history broke every record for length and depth. He continued to study, earning a master's degree in 1952 and a Ph.D. in history two years later.

Kissinger loved Harvard University and took a job directing the Harvard International Seminar, a prestigious program that brought many important international leaders to Cambridge, Massachusetts. He stayed in the position from 1952 to 1969. During this time, Kissinger also became involved with the Council on Foreign Relations, a group that debated and analyzed U.S. policies in relation to the world. Kissinger wrote a book, *Nuclear Weapons and Foreign Policy,* in which he discussed his belief that the threat of nuclear weapons could be used to maintain peace and stability in the world.

Over the next several years, Kissinger became deeply involved with the war being fought in Vietnam. Communists in the north of the country were attempting to take control of the government. The United States would never have become involved in such a civil war had not larger issues been at stake. Following World War II, the Communist Soviet Union grew in military power. Many people believed the ultimate goal of the Soviets was to take over the world. Such a takeover, many argued, would happen gradually, one country at a time until all had fallen. Kissinger and many others believed Communism had to be stopped in small countries like Vietnam if it was to be prevented from spreading everywhere. Kissinger argued that the United States and the Soviet Union were the world's two superpowers and that they were enemies. All U.S. policies, he claimed, ought to be shaped with this in mind.

In 1972, thanks to Kissinger's secret negotiations with the Chinese government, President Richard Nixon made history as the first U.S. president to visit Communist China. Kissinger believed that formal relations with China would make the Soviet Union think twice before launching any sort of military strike against China or the United States.

Few were surprised when in 1973, President Nixon named Kissinger his secretary of state. The secretary of state is in charge of all of the nation's dealings with foreign governments. Kissinger had spent his entire life preparing for this role and he quickly became one of the president's most trusted advisers. Kissinger could not have entered the White House at a more challenging time. The war in Vietnam had dragged on for more than a decade. Day after day, American and foreign soldiers died. Most Americans desperately wanted an end to the war.

The Vietnam era was a terrible chapter in United States history, and Nixon had run for the presidency on a promise to end U.S. involvement in it. Many U.S. military actions were highly questionable during these years. Nixon and Kissinger illegally launched a "secret war" in Cambodia, which was later stopped by an act of Congress. Kissinger believed the United States had to maneuver to a position of strength in order to achieve "peace with honor." To this end, Nixon ordered massive bombings and attacks in an attempt to bring the North Vietnamese to their knees. But nothing the United States did seemed to have any effect except to bring more misery to the war-torn country.

Finally, in 1973, following extremely difficult negotiations, Kissinger signed a cease-fire agreement with North Vietnamese representative Le Duc Tho. At last the terrible war would end. For his efforts, Kissinger shared the 1973 Nobel Peace Prize with Le Duc Tho, the highest honor a diplomat can receive.

Kissinger also sought peace in the Middle East. He began a practice still in use today called "shuttle diplomacy." It was quite common for Kissinger to fly to Israel to discuss peace plans with Israeli leaders, then to fly immediately to Egypt to speak with Arab representatives. It was Kissinger, along with courageous Egyptian president Anwar Sadat, who laid the groundwork for peace between Egypt and Israel.

In addition to his active roles in the major world events of the 1970s, Henry Kissinger was witness to the darkest event in American political history. As Richard Nixon's trusted adviser, Kissinger could only watch as Nixon's presidency crumbled in the fallout from the Watergate scandal of 1973. Nixon resigned from the presidency in disgrace in 1974, the first U.S. president to do so.

Kissinger, however, stayed in the White House and worked as secretary of state for the next president, Gerald Ford. In his career, Kissinger will be remembered as a man who was forced to make difficult choices. He made such choices using his brilliant mind more than his heart, and he always chose the most practical solution. Kissinger will always be remembered as one of the most important shapers of American foreign policy after World War II, a time when the United States has enjoyed unprecedented prosperity and power. Perhaps most significantly, Kissinger's notion of strength in dealing with the Soviet Union during the 1970s played a large part in contributing to the collapse of Communism during the 1980s.

Elie Wiesel

Elie Wiesel has written more than thirty-five books. Still, to call Wiesel an "author" does not do justice to his life's work. He might better be called a "witness." He was witness to a crime so huge and so evil that it looms beyond human understanding. As the world's most recognized Holocaust survivor, Elie Wiesel has succeeded in reporting this crime to the world and making sure that new generations will know the truth.

Eliezar Wiesel was the third child and only son of Shlomo and Sarah Wiesel. Shlomo was a grocer and community leader in their town of Sighet,

Romania. Elie was a very bright boy, interested in psychology, astronomy, and Hebrew. His father encouraged him in his studies of these disciplines while his mother taught him to love the Torah and Talmud, sacred Jewish texts. Elie was a quiet, pious young man, a student who thought little about what went on in the world around him. He might have ended up a rabbi in Sighet or some nearby Jewish village. But by the time Wiesel was ten years old, a series of frightening events had taken place in Europe.

Beginning in 1936, members of the Nazi party in Germany had looted Jewish businesses and burned synagogues. Jews were beaten and killed by thugs in brown uniforms. Soon, the leader of these Nazi "brown-shirts," Adolf Hitler, rose to become the dictatorial ruler of Germany. In 1939, Hitler's tanks invaded Poland. Hearing of such devastating events, many Jews in Romania and other Eastern European countries were deeply frightened. Many wanted to emigrate to Great Britain or the United States. But Shlomo Wiesel counseled against doing anything rash. He believed the Germans would be stopped, and the terrible things happening in Poland and Germany would never happen in their quiet Romanian town. Sadly, he was wrong. As the months passed, no army could stop the Nazis from sweeping across Europe. On Passover week in April 1944, all of Sighet's Jews were rounded up by soldiers, arrested, and moved to a secured area of the town.

On June 13, 1944, a week after the Allied forces had begun the huge D-Day attack that would at last lead to Germany's defeat, Sighet's Jews were ordered to line up in the street with all their belongings. One can hardly imagine the absolute terror these citizens must have felt. By then, they all knew what a journey to a concentration camp meant. Slavery, torture by sadistic guards, starvation, disease, and death awaited them. The Wiesel family was not chosen to board the trains that arrived that first day. Instead, they were locked inside the town's synagogue as prisoners of the Nazis. A week later, the Wiesels were put on the last of the trains to leave

Sighet. Elie, his parents, and his three sisters were taken to Poland. For two days they traveled, crammed into boxcars with no water, food, or sanitary facilities. At last, they arrived at a camp called Auschwitz-Birkenau.

Here, Elie Wiesel would see things nearly impossible to believe. One night, following an Allied bombing raid on the camp, the Nazi guards hung three randomly selected Jewish men as punishment. Wiesel, still just a boy, stood staring at the three innocent men hanging dead, their hands bound behind them. Then he looked at the men who had committed these murders. How, he wondered, could human beings be so cruel to other human beings? How could the loving God Wiesel had read about in the Torah allow such things to occur? It was at this moment that the young, pious student lost his faith. The foundation upon which his whole world had been built seemed to him a lie. The only thing that was real was the need to survive. He realized he must focus on surviving from one day to the next.

In January 1945, the Nazis were being defeated on the battlefield, but in concentration camps, they continued to massacre Jews, Gypsies, political prisoners, homosexuals, Jehovah's Witnesses—anyone perceived by them to be "impure." Fearful that U.S., British, and Soviet soldiers would soon liberate Auschwitz, authorities at the camp decided to "liquidate" the remaining prisoners by forcing them to march until they died of starvation and disease. Shlomo Wiesel, already weak from illness, could barely walk. Fifteen-year-old Elie did all he could to keep his dying father moving. Any marcher who stopped was beaten or simply shot by guards. Though his own foot was badly infected, Elie Wiesel helped carry his father mile after mile. At last, his father could go no further and died during the night. When he found that his father had died, Elie Wiesel felt no sorrow. Instead, he was faced with a feeling of relief—he would not have to carry his father any further. Never would Elie forget the terrible guilt associated with that relief.

Eventually, Allied forces liberated Wiesel and his fellow Auschwitz survivors. Wiesel said of the soldiers: "They were the first free men to see the world of horror. I'll never forget their eyes, the rage, the anger. This reaction was so profound. We became each others' witnesses." Of the Wiesel family, only Elie and his two older sisters, Beatrice and Hilda, survived. Wiesel's parents and baby sister were murdered.

Still only eighteen years old, Wiesel moved to France and began studying philosophy. He was searching for answers, reasons. "I was not eighteen. I was an old man," he wrote much later. "What I knew then, the teachers of my teachers never knew. What I lived in an hour, people don't live in a generation." He did his best to put the past behind him. He made no effort to write about his experiences: what could one say, after all? How could one find the right words to describe what he had seen?

In Paris during the 1950s, Wiesel made a living tutoring students, directing a choir, and translating articles and books. He worked as a journalist, often writing for Jewish newspapers. But he could not muster the strength to speak about the Holocaust. It took Wiesel ten years to break his silence. In 1956, his book *And the World Remained Silent* was published in Argentina. In 1960, he published *Night,* a chilling but beautifully written description of his time at Auschwitz and the final march he made with his father. Since its publication, millions of young people around the world have read *Night* as their introduction to the story of the Holocaust.

Wiesel became a United States citizen in 1963. In 1964, he published *The Town Beyond the Wall.* The novel was about his imagined return to his home village of Sighet. Following the book's publication, Wiesel actually made the emotional journey back to his homeland.

In the 1960s and 1970s, Elie Wiesel served as an international spokesperson on issues concerning human rights throughout the world. In 1965, his book *The Jews of Silence* helped pressure the Soviet government to allow persecuted Jews to emigrate to Israel and the United States. He has spoken

At the dedication of the U.S. Holocaust Memorial Museum, Elie Wiesel (right) joined with President Bill Clinton (center) in lighting an eternal flame outside the museum.

and written on behalf of victims of famine in Ethiopia, Indians suffering oppression in Nicaragua, Cambodian boat people, and missing children believed murdered by the Argentine government.

Wiesel married another Holocaust survivor, Marion Rose, in 1969. They had a son and named him Shlomo Eliezar in memory of Wiesel's father. During his lifetime, Wiesel has been awarded the U.S. Congressional Medal of Honor, the Martin Luther King Award, and in 1986, the Nobel Peace Prize. Wiesel, as a professor, lecturer, and writer acts as a conscience for the United States and the world. In 1987, when President Reagan announced he would visit a German cemetery where many especially vicious Nazi soldiers were buried, Wiesel argued forcefully that such an action disgraced the United States and sullied the memory of the murdered millions. Though Reagan ultimately ignored Wiesel's pleas, the incident became an embarrassment to his presidency.

Ultimately, Elie Wiesel's heroism came after he survived life in Auschwitz. Seeing what he had seen, suffering what he suffered, he might easily have decided simply that humanity, capable of such terrible evil, could not be saved. But he did not give up on the world. "The opposite of love is not hate, it is indifference," he has said. "The opposite of life is not death, but indifference to life and death." Instead of withdrawing from the world and ignoring the pain of others because his own is so great, Wiesel has dedicated his life to fighting against the indifference that allows terrible acts to be committed. Elie Wiesel stands as one of the most righteous leaders of the twentieth century.

Few figures command such respect worldwide. People often think of Elie Wiesel alongside luminaries such as Nelson Mandela, Mother Theresa, and Martin Luther King, Jr. In 1978, President Jimmy Carter appointed Wiesel as chairman of a U.S. Holocaust Memorial council. The council was challenged with building a national memorial that would not only honor the victims of the Holocaust, but would educate society about the Holocaust. Led by Wiesel, the council decided to build a museum in Washington, D.C., that would serve this purpose. Opened on April 22, 1993, the U.S. Holocaust Memorial Museum immediately became one of the most-visited sites in Washington. Scholarship, education, and remembrance of the murdered make this museum a place filled with profound sorrow, but also hope. One could say the same of Elie Wiesel's remarkable life and work.

Maurice Sendak

CHILDREN'S AUTHOR
1928–

Maurice Sendak is among the most popular American authors. His classic book *Where the Wild Things Are* is treasured by millions of people throughout the world. But Sendak does not think of himself as a writer of children's books. "I certainly am not conscious of sitting down and writing a book for children. I think it would be fatal if one did. So I write books and I hope they are books that anyone can read."

It was probably Sendak's childhood that shaped him into a storyteller and artist. The youngest of three children born to Philip and Sarah Sendak in Brooklyn, New

York, Maurice was a sickly boy who often could not go outside to play. He spent many hours staring dreamily out the window at neighborhood boys and girls playing games, running, and jumping. "I was miserable as a kid. I couldn't make friends. I couldn't play stoopball terrific. I couldn't skate great. I stayed home and drew pictures. You know what they all thought of me—sissy Maurice Sendak. When I wanted to go out and do something, my father would say, 'You'll catch cold!' And I did . . . I did whatever he told me."

Maurice loved listening to his father tell stories from Jewish folklore. The magical stories stayed in Maurice's mind and fired his imagination. But when his older sister bought him his first book, *The Prince and the Pauper* by Mark Twain, it was not so much the story that Sendak liked, but the book itself. He vividly remembers its shiny cover and the pleasure he took in smelling its pages: "It was just a beautiful object." The book looked and felt so good that Maurice even tried to bite it! "I don't imagine that's what my sister intended when she bought the book for me! But I think it started then, a passion for books and book making."

In high school, Sendak was not a particularly strong student. He tended to daydream and was lazy in his studies. But he could draw. In fact, while still in high school, Sendak got a job turning the newspaper comic strip "Mutt and Jeff" into a comic book. When Sendak graduated from high school, he got a new job creating life-size storybook characters out of papier-mâché. Two years later, he got a promotion, but he found his new position boring and soon quit. Sendak had no trouble keeping busy. He and his brother Jack began a new project. Together, they built intricate and beautiful moving figures out of wood and clockwork. Jack created the mechanical parts, and Maurice did all the painting and carving.

The brothers took their creations to F.A.O. Schwarz, a famous New York toy store, in hopes of selling them. The store's buyer thought the toys were magnificent, but explained that mass-producing them would be too expensive. Another employee of the store, the man in charge of creating window displays, saw Maurice's painting and design ability and hired him on the spot.

Sendak might have remained with F.A.O. Schwarz for many years had his co-workers not secretly sent some of his drawings to a children's publisher. In 1952, Sendak was chosen to illustrate *A Hole is To Dig.* The book became a huge hit and today is considered a classic of children's literature, thanks in large part to Sendak's drawings. Many illustrators began imitating Sendak's unique drawing style. Sendak had found his life's work. But he wasn't happy with drawing the pictures for someone else's story. He wanted to write a book of his own. In 1955, he wrote *Kenny's Window.* The book was a good first effort, but Sendak was ultimately dissatisfied with it.

In the early 1960s he decided to write a book based more on pictures than on text. The result was *Where the Wild Things Are,* one of the most popular children's books of all time. It has sold millions of copies and has been translated into thirteen languages. When it was released in 1964, the book won many awards, including the distinguished Caldecott Medal.

Where the Wild Things Are was popular, but it was also very controversial. The book's main character is a little boy named Max. Dressed in a wolf suit, Max misbehaves and is sent to bed without any supper. This enrages the little boy. "I'll eat you up," Max tells his mother. Soon, when Max is alone, trees grow from the bedposts and readers are taken into a magic forest "where the wild things are." Some parents and child-care professionals believed children might get the wrong message from the story. Max acted like a real little boy, rather than the sort of perfect little children usually found in books for boys and girls. A *New York Times* reviewer claimed that was precisely the genius of Sendak's book: "Maurice Sendak shouts a resounding 'No!' to the idea there is something inherently good about a tidy, obedient child." Children loved the book because it dealt with real feelings they experienced each day.

In the end, Max returns from the forest to "where someone loves him best of all," and finds his dinner waiting for him—"And it was still hot." The feelings of anger give way to forgiveness and the knowledge that Max's mother loves him and he loves his mother. It is likely Sendak's depiction of conflicting and changing feelings that makes children love his books. Sendak acknowledges that children are human beings, just like adults. "Children know a lot more than people give them credit for," he has said. "Children are willing to deal with many dubious subjects that grown-ups think they shouldn't know about. But children are small courageous people who have to deal every day with a multitude of problems, just as we adults do."

Soon after the huge success of *Where the Wild Things Are,* Sendak suffered a series of sad events in his life. First, his mother died of cancer. The two had been very close, and he missed her a great deal. Then, just a few months later, his beloved dog Jennie had to be put to sleep at the age of fourteen. For a long time, he did not feel like writing or drawing. In 1967, he wrote *Higgelty, Piggelty, Pop!* and dedicated it to Jennie.

Always experimenting with new ideas, Sendak writes hundreds of drafts of each book before settling on a final version. He often works for years on a text of only 300 or 400 words. Such dedication has paid off. Maurice Sendak has won numerous awards around the world. In 1983, he was honored with the Association for Library Service to Children Award for his "substantial and lasting contribution to Children's Literature." Today, his books are being given to children by parents who themselves grew up with Sendak's stories and illustrations. And it seems likely that today's children will pass them on to a third generation of boys and girls.

Beverly Sills

OPERA SINGER AND ADMINISTRATOR
1929–

Beverly Sills was born Belle Miriam Silverman in Brooklyn, New York. Three years later, she was named "Brooklyn's Most Beautiful Baby of 1932." Though her father had dreamed his daughter would one day teach school, she was in show business to stay. By age four, "Bubbles" was singing on various local radio shows. At age seven, she sang in a movie and had already memorized twenty-two opera arias by listening to her parents' record collection. Estelle Liebling, a famous voice teacher, took Sills on as a pupil during her sophomore year in high school. While studying singing, Sills also took up the piano and quickly learned to play the instrument well enough to play professionally. In 1938, she sang on the popular television program *Major Bowe's Capitol Family Hour.*

In fact, by the time she graduated from P.S. 91 in Brooklyn, future stardom seemed assured. Her classmates named her "Prettiest Girl," "Fashion Plate," the "One With the Most Personality," and "Most Likely to Succeed." Beverly went to a high school for children working in the entertainment field, and by age fifteen, she had learned to sing twenty different opera roles, an incredible musical accomplishment at any age. Just four years later, she had learned more than fifty different roles! Sills established herself as more than simply a child star. She was a musical prodigy.

In 1945, Sills accepted an offer to join a touring company that performed the light operas of Gilbert and Sullivan. Still only sixteen years old, she became known as the "youngest prima donna in captivity." The opera world began to take notice of the pretty and vivacious young soprano. In 1947, she was cast as Frasquita, a major role in the opera *Carmen,* in a Philadelphia Opera Company production.

Sills sang many other roles during the 1950s for various American opera companies. Her big break came in 1955, when she first appeared with the New York Ciy Opera. Her magnificent voice had reached full maturity. Still, Sills continued to work hard to improve as a musician and had learned one hundred different roles. At her peak, she performed 100 times a year, singing 60 different roles. Her amazing memory allowed her to know all the parts in every opera in which she performed. This deep knowledge of each opera's music and story enabled her to become a splendid actress as well as a great opera singer. In 1953, she became a full member of the New York City Opera (NYCO) and would do much to make the NYCO into a world-class company.

In 1956, Sills took a brief break from her busy schedule to get married to Peter Buckeley Greenough, the associate editor of the Cleveland *Plain*

Dealer newspaper. Greenough and Sills had two children. Sadly, their daughter was born deaf, and their second child, a son, was profoundly retarded. When the boy was six, Sills was forced to place him in an institution where he would receive professional care twenty-four hours a day. Sills began wearing two watches as she traveled throughout the world. She kept one set on her son's schedule so that she could always imagine what he was doing at a given moment. In 1972, Sills served as the national chairperson for the Mother's March on Birth Defects.

As Sills became more famous, she used her new power to promote the work of lesser-known opera composers. By the mid-1960s, Beverly Sills had become widely known as perhaps the greatest opera singer in the United States. Oddly, she had never given a formal debut performance with the nation's most prominent opera company. A long-standing feud with the director of New York's Metropolitan Opera Company kept her from singing there until 1975. The clash was a boon to many smaller companies who were able to hire the great star even after she had become world famous. In the long run, this was great for American opera. Many people, upon hearing that the star was coming to their city, bought tickets to see an opera for the first time.

After dominating the opera stage through the 1960s and 1970s, Beverly Sills decided to retire from performing in 1980. She accepted a job as general director of the New York City Opera Company, which she held until 1989. Her charm and personality, as well as her skill as a promoter and administrator, did much to strengthen that organization and opera in general. In 1994, Sills was elected the chairperson of Lincoln Center in New York, a fund-raising and policy-making position of great power in the performing arts. Sills's marvelous soprano voice and great musicianship, along with her winning personality, helped establish a serious audience for opera in the United States and cleared the way for other American singers to gain a world audience.

Ruth Bader Ginsburg

SUPREME COURT JUSTICE
1933 –

In 1993, Ruth Bader Ginsburg became just the second woman ever to be named a justice on the United States Supreme Court. This was the crowning achievement of a long and important legal career during which Ginsburg was a major force in the fight for women's rights.

Ruth Bader was born in Brooklyn, New York, to Nathan and Celia Bader. Her father ran a men's clothing store. Even as a schoolgirl, Ruth Bader noticed that her mother, though as intelligent and capable as any man she knew, never had a chance to work outside the home. Many years later, in accepting her Supreme Court appointment, Ginsburg talked about her mother: "I pray that I may be all that she would have been had she lived in an age when women could aspire and achieve, and daughters would be cherished as much as sons."

In 1954, Ruth Bader married a lawyer named Martin Ginsburg and decided to add his name to hers. That same year, she also graduated from Cornell University and was accepted to the prestigious Law School at Harvard University. Ginsburg was one of only 9 women in a class of 500 students. Later, when her husband got a job in New York, Ginsburg decided to transfer to Columbia University Law School; she graduated in 1959.

Ginsburg had been a brilliant student at both Harvard and Columbia. Even though she graduated first in her class at Columbia, none of New York's important law firms would hire her. Women simply were not accepted as lawyers. In 1960, one of her Harvard professors recommended she be allowed to clerk for Supreme Court Justice Felix Frankfurter. To clerk for a Supreme Court justice is an honor, and Frankfurter was a respected and renowned member of the court. Frankfurter examined Ginsburg's record and agreed she was qualified for the job. But he chose not to hire Ginsburg and explained he just was not ready to hire a woman! This was a turning point in Ginsburg's life. As time wore on, disappointment gave way to deep anger, and Ginsburg became determined to do all she could to raise the station of women in society. Rather than succumbing to disgust and frustration, Ginsburg channeled her anger into strong action. She took every slight, every unfair practice, as a chance to advance the cause of equality.

Ginsburg accepted a job as a clerk for a district court judge in New York, then taught at Rutgers University. While at Rutgers, Ginsburg became pregnant with her second child. She was forced to hide her pregnancy to avoid university policies requiring pregnant women to give up their jobs. Ginsburg would later help reform the laws governing such practices. In

1972, Ginsburg taught a course on women and the law at Harvard University Law School. She was offered a position at Harvard, but without tenure. Tenure guarantees a professor will not be fired based on his or her political beliefs. Unwilling to accept "second-class" status on the Harvard faculty, she declined the offer. In 1973, Columbia University offered her a fully tenured position which she accepted.

An excellent teacher and scholar, Ginsburg wanted to do more to advance the cause of women's rights. So she became a lawyer with the American Civil Liberties Union (ACLU). The ACLU helps protect the constitutional rights of U.S. citizens. During the 1970s, the ACLU became involved in many women's rights issues. Instead of attempting sweeping change, Ginsburg decided it was best to work within the legal system, methodically fighting law after law that discriminated against women and other groups.

In 1973, Ginsburg argued her first case before the Supreme Court. Federal law at the time allowed more housing and medical benefits to men in the military than to women. The law further discriminated against military families in which women soldiers earned the bulk of the income. Ginsburg claimed that the law not only disadvantaged men who were dependent upon their wives' salaries, but also minimized the contribution of women in the armed forces. She won the case. Soon thereafter she saw to it that laws giving various social security benefits to widows but not to widowers were struck down as unfair, too. She did the same to an Oklahoma law stating that women could purchase alcoholic beverages at age eighteen, while men were required to be twenty-one. By attacking laws that treated women or men differently or unfairly based on their gender, Ginsburg based the cause of women's rights on reason, rather than emotion. Her argument was always that the law could not grant rights to one group and not to another. Ginsburg went on to win five of the six cases she argued before the Supreme Court, more victories than any other lawyer in history.

In 1980, President Jimmy Carter named Ginsburg a judge on the U.S. Court of Appeals for Washington, D.C. In her role as judge, Ginsburg was less vocal in her support of women's rights. She believed a judge had a different role than a lawyer. A judge's job is to interpret the laws made by elected officials, rather than to decide whether those laws are fair. Often, she angered people who had been on her side. For instance, many African-American leaders were displeased with her stand against affirmative action. Such programs grant African-Americans special opportunities for education and jobs. She claimed such practices demeaned the achievements of blacks who had succeeded when allowed to compete on an equal basis with whites.

Ginsburg remained a scholar who examined the fine points of the law with great care. As a judge, she became widely known for her brilliant questioning of lawyers arguing cases before her, and her ability to reason with those who opposed her ideas. Clearly these strengths were foremost in President Bill Clinton's mind when he chose Ginsburg to succeed retiring Supreme Court Justice Byron White. Clinton said, "I believe that in the years ahead, she will be able to be a force for consensus-building on the Supreme Court, just as she has been on the Court of Appeals, so that our judges can become an instrument of our common unity in the expression of their fidelity to the Constitution."

After the Senate confirmed Ginsburg's nomination by a vote of ninety-six in favor and only three opposed, Senator Joseph Biden said that during her career Ginsburg had "helped to change the meaning of equality in our nation." On August 10, 1993, Ruth Bader Ginsburg was sworn in as the 107th Supreme Court justice. As only the second woman ever to hold the position, she is well aware that work remains to be done if women are to enjoy meaningful equality in the United States. Ginsburg has done much to advance that worthy cause.

Dianne Feinstein

UNITED STATES SENATOR

1933–

Dianne Feinstein's father was a doctor, and he enjoyed bringing her along on his rounds at the hospital. He hoped his little girl would one day grow up to be a surgeon just like him. But Dianne found the sights, sounds, and smells of the ward unpleasant. She preferred the walks her Uncle Morris took her on through the streets of San Francisco. He was a business-man and a Democratic Party supporter who loved to talk to people. "Everything I learned about politics I learned from my Uncle Morris. He's the one who taught me that people will talk to you if you will listen."

Feinstein's childhood was difficult. Her mother suffered from a rare brain disorder that made her behave strangely, often violently. Once, her mother chased her around the house waving a carving knife. On the night before her college entrance exams, Feinstein's mother threw her out of the house. She was forced to sleep in the garage. Still, she scored well enough to be admitted to Stanford University, one of the finest universities in the country. "I did not have a terrible childhood," Feinstein once said. "Some terrible things happened, but I did not have a terrible childhood."

Following a fine career at Stanford, Feinstein took a position on the California Women's Parole Board. In 1969, Feinstein was elected to the San Francisco Board of Supervisors, the first woman ever so honored. Feinstein became deeply concerned with the problems of the poor and worked hard to try and solve them. She made frequent trips to high-crime neighborhoods to meet and talk with young people. Community activists praised her willingness to attack difficult problems head-on whether or not it earned her greater popularity. She also helped forge stronger bonds between various individuals and groups dedicated to serving disadvantaged citizens. Such had not been the case with other politicians.

During the next several years, Feinstein twice ran for mayor and lost. The experience reminded her a bit of the time she ran for vice president of her class at Stanford University. She had wanted to run for president but decided that she had no chance of winning. "I stood on the Quad, talking to people, and I found out they would rather elect a monkey, a giraffe, or an ant before they would elect a woman."

In 1978, Feinstein decided to retire from politics. She had worked in state and city government in California for eighteen years. On November 27, reporters gathered at City Hall to hear her announcement. Two hours later, those same reporters were back at City Hall to cover a shocking and tragic event. Mayor George Moscone and Supervisor Harvey Milk had been gunned down by another supervisor. Feinstein rushed down the hall to the scene of the crime and held Harvey Milk in her arms as he died.

Still president of the Board of Supervisors, Feinstein became interim mayor. She was the first woman ever to hold that office. Feinstein's first job as mayor was to announce the deaths of Moscone and Milk. "I feel a very great need to heal and bind," she told reporters. In the weeks following the murders, Feinstein did much to heal the emotionally wounded city of San Francisco.

In 1979, Feinstein was elected to a full term as mayor of San Francisco. She had become known as a strong advocate for minorities, women, and the poor, while at the same time being tough on crime and in favor of expanding business opportunities in the city. She also faced the problem of AIDS, which hit San Francisco particularly hard due to its large gay population. Feinstein helped put together a strong program to battle the disease's spread.

In 1987, Feinstein left office because she had completed her second term as mayor, the city's limit. That year the Women's International Center presented her with a Living Legacy Award. Asked how she hoped to be remembered, she said, "As a mayor who did her best to make San Francisco a better place to live, provided fiscal stability and vital public services, improved management within local government and created an effective role model for women in executive positions."

Feinstein was hospitalized in 1989 for medical complications following a hysterectomy but felt strong enough in 1990 to run for governor of California. She lost a hard-fought campaign to Republican Pete Wilson. Feinstein learned much from the defeat. She ran a stronger campaign in 1992 and was elected to the United States Senate in what became known as "The Year of the Woman." That same year Barbara Boxer (also a Jewish American) was elected as California's other senator.

Once in the Senate, Feinstein continued to voice her beliefs. Facing a tough Republican majority, Feinstein fought to preserve social programs that helped poor families. Perhaps her biggest accomplishment was her sponsorship of the Desert Preservation Act. The act created a protected wilderness area of 6 million acres (2 million hectares) in California, Arizona, and New Mexico. Two new national parks in Death Valley and Joshua Tree were established along with the Mojave National Preserve. Feinstein was reelected to the Senate in 1994 and has continued to fight for the rights of those without money or power.

Larry King

TALK SHOW HOST
1933 –

When Larry King was a boy, he would sit and listen to the radio for hours. He stared intently at the glowing dial and dreamed of a day when his own voice would be heard in homes throughout the country.

Born Lawrence Zeigler, King grew up in Brooklyn, New York, where his parents ran a popular restaurant. They were devout Jews and kept a kosher home. During World War II, King's father sold the restaurant and took a job helping the war effort at a factory in New Jersey. This new job would change the course of young Larry's life. In 1944, when Larry was just ten years old, his father suffered a heart attack and died while working at the defense plant. The family was soon forced to accept government welfare payments to survive.

His father's death destroyed Larry's faith in god and turned him into a troublemaker at school. When Larry graduated from Lafayette High School in 1951, his grades were poor and his teachers feared he would never make anything of himself. He spent most of his time at Brooklyn Dodger games or listening to the radio. Arthur Godfrey, Walter Winchell, and Bob and Ray were his favorite radio personalities. Such stars seemed incredibly glamorous and important. Larry longed to be among them.

Following graduation, he took a job as a delivery boy, then became a mail clerk. In the spring of 1957, a friend advised him to go to Miami because there was an opening at a radio station there. At the age of twenty-three, Larry Ziegler immediately headed south in the belief that his big break would come quickly. At first, he had a job sweeping floors at a Miami station. But even this made him happy. His career in radio had begun.

As he cleaned and did odd jobs around the station Zeigler let everybody know that his ambition was to be on the air. Finally, he got his chance. When a disk jockey quit suddenly one morning, the station manager decided to "give the kid a shot." A few minutes before airtime, the station manager told Zeigler his name was "a little . . . ethnic." The station manager glanced at a newspaper ad for a store called King's Wholesale Liquors. "How about Larry King?" he suggested. King or Zeigler—it made no difference to Larry so long as he had his own show.

Larry King's career took off a few years later when a Miami restaurant called Pumpernik's hired him to do a four-hour show from its dining room. The show was simple. King chatted with whomever happened to walk in for breakfast. Soon celebrities and unknowns began coming to the restaurant hoping to get on King's show. Among those who got their start on the program were young comedians Don Rickles and Lenny Bruce, and pop singer Bobby Darin. The show became popular with listeners due to King's smooth interviewing style. By 1964, King was appearing on television as well as radio, and a year later he began writing a column for a Miami newspaper. By 1966, King's various jobs in the media had made him a wealthy man.

Money and fame soon led to problems for King. "At my most egotistical moments," he wrote later in his autobiography, "I felt as if I owned Miami." He bought expensive cars, fancy clothes, and gambled away a lot of money on horses at the racetrack. His life began to spin out of control. Then King became friends with Louis Wolfson, a wealthy financier. In 1968, Wolfson gave King five thousand dollars to pass on to a man named Jim Garrison. Garrison, the district attorney for New Orleans, planned to use the money to aid in his investigation of John F. Kennedy's assassination. Deep in debt and desperate, King used the money to pay his own tax bill. Wolfson had King arrested. Eventually, all charges were dropped, but King's reputation was ruined along with his career in the media. He lost his job as a commentator for the Miami Dolphins football team, his local television talk show, his newspaper column, and his disk jockey position.

By 1978, King was forced to declare bankruptcy as he owed more than $300,000 to creditors. That same year, however, King got a second chance in radio. The Mutual Broadcasting Network offered him a national, late-night talk show in Washington, D.C. The show was heard in 28 cities to start, but soon was carried by more than 250 stations across the United States. King had a weekly audience of five million listeners. The show won the prestigious George Foster Peabody Award in 1982, the first talk show ever so honored. Today, the *Guinness Book of World Records* lists Larry King as having logged more hours on radio than anyone else in history.

In 1985, CNN hired King to host a live television call-in show, "Larry King Live." The move to television doubled his pay, and because CNN was beamed around the world, King became an international figure. His position of influence was cemented in 1992 when Ross Perot announced his run for the presidency on the show. Soon, "Larry King Live" became known for attracting celebrities and people in the news who did not normally consent to interviews. King's big catches range from President Bill Clinton to reclusive actor Marlon Brando.

King avoids knowing much about his guests before they appear on the show. Instead, he relies on his natural curiosity to make for a good interview. "The less I know in advance, the more curious I am on the air." His curiosity leads him to ask the questions viewers want asked. Larry King's strong personality and probing questions have made "Larry King Live" the most-watched talk show in the world. The show's popularity made his autobiography *Larry King by Larry King* a national best-seller.

King has been married seven times and has one daughter. In 1987, he suffered a heart attack and underwent open-heart surgery. Today, he is in good health and as popular as ever. In 1995, he returned triumphantly to his hometown of Brooklyn where he was crowned "King of Brooklyn" in front of a cheering crowd.

Gloria Steinem

WOMEN'S RIGHTS ADVOCATE
1 9 3 4 –

Gloria Steinem was among the most famous and most vocal leaders of the women's movement in the 1970s. Intelligent and provocative, both loved and hated by the popular press and the public, Steinem has worked for a lifetime on behalf of women and oppressed people around the world.

Steinem's father was an antique dealer, and her mother was a journalist. Neither managed to make a very good living. When Gloria was a girl, the family spent several years traveling across the United States in a trailer. This exposure to a huge variety of people and places changed the way she thought about the world. She came to appreciate diversity and learned that most people wanted the same things: a decent home, a job, and family life. When Gloria was eleven, her parents divorced, and she was to learn just how valuable these things were. Gloria and her mother lived in poverty for several years. In addition, her mother suffered from depression, an ordeal Steinem later described in a memoir titled *Ruth's Song (Because She Could Not Sing It)*. "She was just a fact of life growing up," she wrote of her mother, "someone to be worried about and cared for; an invalid who lay in bed with eyes closed and lips moving in occasional response to voices only she could hear." At age fifteen, Gloria was sent to Washington, D.C., to live with her older sister. Suffering under terrible stress, Gloria's high school grades were poor, but her exceptional college entrance exam scores gained her a place at Smith College, a prestigious women's school, in 1952.

At Smith, relieved of the burdens of home, Steinem showed tremendous promise. In 1956, she graduated magna cum laude and Phi Beta Kappa, among the highest honors a graduating college student can receive. On the strength of such achievements, she won a fellowship to study in India for two years. She found India to be a magnificent place but one filled with terrible poverty and suffering. Once again, the way she viewed the world changed. She said later, "America is an enormous frosted cupcake in the middle of millions of starving people."

Determined to work to raise the status of oppressed people, Steinem realized early on that simply protesting and shouting did little to change people's minds. First, one had to get their attention. Steinem became famous when she took a job as a Playboy "bunny" and wrote about the experience for a magazine. Playboy bunnies wore skimpy costumes and served as cocktail waitresses at Playboy clubs throughout the United States. Steinem found the conditions the Playboy bunnies worked under to be deplorable and demeaning. In 1970, she and Playboy's president, Hugh Hefner, published a long debate in his magazine in which they discussed the issues she had raised about his clubs, and the cause of women's rights in general. Gloria Steinem became a household name and a spokesperson for the women's movement. Many saw her as a hero, others thought her assault on traditional values would ruin the country.

During the next several years, Steinem supported various political candidates from the Democratic Party. She joined those protesting the war in Vietnam and spoke out on the life-threatening problems caused by a lack of legal abortion services in the United States. In 1971, Steinem, Bella Abzug, Shirley Chisholm, and author Betty Friedan formed the National Women's Political Caucus. The organization aimed to inspire more women to run for elected office and helped lay the groundwork for the many women holding public office today.

Perhaps Steinem's most important contribution to the women's movement came in 1972, when she helped found *Ms.*, a magazine that examined issues from a feminist slant. The first major publication of its kind, the circulation of *Ms.* quickly soared to a half-million, and the magazine helped to sway public opinion. Women across the country felt empowered by the magazine's strong feminist stance. Throughout the 1970s and 1980s, Steinem remained a leader of the women's rights movement, speaking throughout the country, and writing articles for various publications. In 1983, she collected many of her essays in *Outrageous Acts and Everyday Rebellions*. Her 1994 book *Moving Beyond Words* examines the modern women's movement.

Gloria Steinem remains one of the more recognizable and important public figures in the United States and still feels passionate about the need to organize people to promote social change: "On a good night, a roomful of people can set off a chain of thought that leads us all to a new place—a sudden explosion of understanding, a spontaneous invention. We hear ourselves saying things we had felt but never named."

Sandy Koufax

BASEBALL PITCHER
1935 –

Jewish Americans have always been especially proud of great Jewish athletes. For Jewish immigrants, such sports heroes seemed proof that they were truly a part of their adopted country. No Jewish athlete ever aroused more pride than Sandy Koufax. As a Brooklyn and Los Angeles Dodger, Koufax rose to become one of the greatest pitchers ever to take the mound.

Koufax was born in 1935 to Jack and Evelyn Braun, who divorced three years later. His mother then married attorney Irving Koufax, who adopted Sandy. While growing up in Brooklyn, New York, Sandy

Koufax began his athletic career. Tall and strong, he was a star forward on the high school basketball team and accepted a college scholarship to play for powerhouse University of Cincinnati. Koufax planned to become an architect after college, and baseball was just a game he played for fun during basketball's off-season.

At the University of Cincinnati, Koufax tried out for the baseball team only when he learned he would get a free trip to California, where the team trained. He soon proved to be an impressive pitcher and attracted attention from major league scouts. As a left-handed starter for the freshman team, Koufax's blistering fastball allowed him to strike out fifty-one batters in just thirty-two innings. The only problem was that he had little idea of where each pitch would go. Such wildness, combined with velocity, made him a frightening pitcher whom few wanted to bat against. But it also made him a risky proposition for major league teams. After all, if a pitcher cannot throw strikes consistently, he will not get major league batters out.

Several teams sent scouts to Cincinnati to watch Koufax throw. Most told him to stick with basketball. The Brooklyn Dodgers, however, decided to gamble on a local product and offered Koufax a hefty signing bonus. Special rules of the time stated that any player signed with a bonus had to immediately join the major league club. So in 1955, still just nineteen years old, Koufax found himself on one of baseball's legendary teams. Among his teammates were the great Jackie Robinson, Duke Snider, and Roy Campanella. Koufax was a raw rookie and would have benefited from time spent in the minors. His manager, Walter Alston, decided the lanky kid with the blazing fastball was too wild to pitch successfully in the major leagues. So until 1959, Koufax rarely pitched during games of any importance.

During these four years, Koufax considered quitting baseball, and many fans and players decided that the so-called "bonus baby" had been a losing bet. But instead of giving up, Koufax kept quiet and tried to learn from the

After missing a start for Yom Kippur, Sandy Koufax led the Dodgers to win the 1965 World Series against the Minnesota Twins.

older players around him. One such player was Norm Sherry, the Dodgers' catcher. Sherry, also Jewish, convinced Koufax he did not need to throw with all his might on every single pitch. Often, Koufax threw marvelously on the sidelines, but upon entering a game constricted his throwing motion by throwing too hard. Sherry advised him to "Have some fun on the mound—throw change-ups and curveballs."

In 1959, that's just what Koufax did, and opposition batters rarely managed to hit the ball hard. Koufax struck out 173 batters in his 153 innings of work. He set a record when he struck out 18 Chicago Cubs in one game.

Koufax's intimidating pitching helped the Dodgers win the National League Pennant and the World Series.

Koufax only got better. For five years, from 1962 through 1966, he was the best pitcher in the game. He won 111 games while losing only 34 and led the league in earned run averages all five seasons. He was always at or near the top of the heap in strikeouts, innings pitched, and complete games. He won 26 games for the Dodgers in the 1965 season, and the following year he won 27.

Casey Stengel, a towering figure of baseball history who spent six decades in the game, claimed that Koufax was the best pitcher he had ever seen. Koufax was awarded the National League Cy Young Award as its best pitcher in 1963, 1965, and 1966. In 1963, Koufax was also named the league's Most Valuable Player. Throughout this time, Koufax was battling painful injuries. During the 1963 season a circulatory problem stopped blood flow to his left index finger. In 1964, he developed arthritis, a serious condition so painful that he only threw a baseball on game days.

Not only was Koufax a great athlete, he was intelligent and a man of principle. When the Dodgers got to the World Series in 1965, Koufax was scheduled to pitch the opening game. The game was to be played on the most sacred Jewish holiday, Yom Kippur. Observant Jews are not allowed to work on Yom Kippur and must worship all day. Koufax, under tremendous pressure to forsake his religious convictions, ignored public pressure. He missed the first game of the World Series in order to attend Yom Kippur services with his parents. Meanwhile, Koufax's replacement, an excellent pitcher named Don Drysdale, had a terrible outing. When Walter Alston went to the mound and took Drysdale out of the game, Drysdale said to his manager, "Bet you wish I was Jewish too!" Many fans criticized Koufax for his decision. But Koufax did not let his team or his fans down. He came back in both the fifth and seventh games to throw shutouts and win the World Series.

Koufax was also among the first players to challenge ownership's unfair labor practices. Until the 1970s, baseball players were forced to either sign a contract with their current team for whatever salary the team offered, or sit out the season. Before the 1966 season, however, Koufax and Drysdale refused to sign their offered contracts. The two reasoned that the Dodgers could not enter the season without their two star pitchers. After a long holdout, the Dodgers gave in and rewarded Koufax with a $130,000 contract.

The Los Angeles Dodgers got their money's worth—Koufax turned in his greatest season. He won twenty-seven games and led the league in every important pitching statistic. Sadly, at the peak of his form, Koufax had to announce his retirement from the game. The arthritis in his pitching elbow threatened to become a crippling problem if he kept playing. For a while, Koufax broadcast games. Later, he became a pitching instructor in the Dodger organization. Today he remains a popular representative of the Dodger organization. Sandy Koufax was inducted into the Baseball Hall of Fame in 1972, the first year he was eligible. He was only thirty-six years old at the time, the youngest man ever to be so honored.

Woody Allen

COMEDIAN, FILMMAKER
1935–

Woody Allen was born Allen Stewart Konigsberg in Brooklyn, New York. His parents, Martin and Nettie, were Orthodox Jews who followed strict Jewish laws and custom. But young Allen "hated every second" of Hebrew school and had little interest in carrying on such traditions. He much preferred baseball, amateur magic, and jazz music. And he was funny. In the movies he has made as an adult, Woody Allen portrays himself as a shy, scrawny, red-haired boy obsessed with a fear of death. He told an interviewer in 1977: "I never ate with the family. And I never did any extracurricular activities at school. [At home] I'd go right to my bedroom and shut the door—immediately. Consequently, I was able to get some things done. I could learn an instrument [the clarinet]. I became adept at sleight of hand, which took me endless hours and which I can still do."

Although he was a poor student, Allen claims always to have been a good writer. "There was never a week when the composition I wrote was not the one read to the class," he boasted in a recent interview. By the time he was in high school, Allen Stewart Konigsberg was able to sell the jokes he wrote in his bedroom when he should have been doing homework. He mailed them into a newspaper under the pen name of Woody Allen. Soon, the world of professional comedy began to take notice of him. By the time he graduated from high school, Woody Allen had been hired to write for television. Sid Caesar's *Your Show of Shows* did not worry that Allen had only recently escaped from high school with a C average. Still only eighteen years old, Woody Allen was working on a writing staff with comic geniuses such as Mel Brooks, Carl Reiner, and Neil Simon.

Allen's parents worried that this success was temporary, and they begged him to attend college. To please them, Allen enrolled in New York University. He was soon expelled for poor grades and absence. One of the many courses he failed at New York University was Motion Picture Production. He later attended—and also flunked out of—City College of New York. Though Allen loved to read and was interested in ideas, he found the atmosphere of formal education stifling. In several of his movies, teachers and professors are portrayed as dull and hypocritical. "Those who can't do, teach. Those who can't teach, teach gym," became one of Woody Allen's most famous lines.

In 1961, Allen made a bold move. Encouraged by friends and a new agent, he quit writing jokes for others and became a performer. Allen molded aspects of his own character into a hilarious monologue. On stage, stuttering and clearing his throat, he discussed his fears of women, death, and mechanical objects. At first, his nervousness and on-stage dread were not an act. The same friends who had encouraged Allen to perform often had to push him into the spotlight. Gradually, Allen gained more confidence as his rich material and endearing shyness got big laughs.

Allen began performing his comedy routine regularly at the Blue Angel, a Manhattan nightclub. In 1964, movie producer Charles Feldman happened to see Allen's act and was so impressed that he immediately hired Allen to write a screenplay for a movie, *What's New, Pussycat?* A farce about spies, the film became a surprise hit and earned more than $17 million at the box office. But Allen thought the movie was an artistic failure. "I never considered that one mine. I hated it, hated working on it, and it was the reason I became a director." Still, the movie's financial success opened the way for Allen to work on many other projects.

His play *Don't Drink the Water* opened on Broadway in 1966 and had a successful run through 1967. *Play it Again, Sam,* another play, starred Allen as a nebbish (a Yiddish word for a nervous wimp) who is helped by the ghost of Humphrey Bogart to impress a woman he loves. (Allen also starred in the 1972 film version of the play.)

By the late 1960s, Woody Allen was a national celebrity. He appeared regularly on television and at comedy clubs throughout the country. Also, he began writing short, humorous articles for *The New Yorker,* a magazine with a distinguished literary history.

Beginning in 1969, Allen made the first of a series of movies that defined his early style of filmmaking. In each of these early films, he played a character that was virtually the same—the nervous, wisecracking guy with glasses—who is placed in unusual situations. The comedy was drawn out of seeing this character (most obviously identified as a Jewish persona) as a bank robber in *Take the Money and Run,* 1969; in the midst of a Latin American revolution in *Bananas,* 1971; and sent into a strange science-fiction future in *Sleeper,* 1973. At this point in his career, Allen has said, he knew little about making films. He simply tried to come up with as many jokes as he could, and filmed them. That same year, he published his first book, *Getting Even,* a collection of his short pieces. He published two more books through the years.

Always pushing himself, Allen decided that his next film would be more artistic. The result was *Love and Death,* in which the same "Woody" character is placed in Russia. Though *Love and Death* contains the usual rapid-fire jokes, it is a far more thoughtful film than his previous work. Allen had begun addressing humankind's and his own deepest fears and questions.

In 1977, Allen wrote and directed *Annie Hall,* which swept Hollywood's Academy Awards, including Best Picture. Allen won Oscars for Best Director, and shared Best Screenplay honors with his co-writer, Marshall Brickman. Diane Keaton, who played the title character, won for Best Actress. The film was a comedy, but it dealt honestly with the difficulties and pain of love and relationships. Allen also made his mark by including many jokes that were based specifically on his Jewish roots and the conflicts that arise over a relationship between a Jewish man and a gentile woman. With the smashing success of *Annie Hall,* Woody Allen had become perhaps the most famous American Jew ever, and one of the most important in that he chose not to hide his Jewishness.

Never content to make the same sort of film twice, Allen experimented continuously. In 1978, he wrote and directed a serious film inspired by Swedish film maker Ingmar Bergman. Though many fans of Allen's early work were perplexed by his sudden shift to drama, *Interiors* received mostly positive reviews and was a modest hit at the box office. Allen was nominated for Best Director. In 1979, Allen portrayed the lives of wealthy Jewish New Yorkers in his sophisticated comedy *Manhattan.* The film was another huge hit, and most critics agreed that it was even better than *Annie Hall.*

Woody Allen on the set of one of his many films

In the two decades since 1977, Allen has created at least one film every year. He has explored all sorts of film styles, from serious drama to fantasy, and even to a musical in 1996. Allen won the Oscar for Best Screenplay for *Hannah and Her Sisters* in 1986, and for *Crimes and Misdemeanors* in 1990. *Crimes and Misdemeanors* reflected Allen's darkest thoughts yet on a society in which murderers go unpunished and human nature too often succumbs to evil out of fear and greed.

The early 1990s were difficult years for Allen as he endured a separation from his longtime companion Mia Farrow and the scandal that erupted when it was revealed that Allen was having an affair with Farrow's adopted teenage daughter. Always intensely private, Allen found his personal life splashed across the front pages of newspapers and magazines around the world. Still, even during this painful period he wrote and directed one of his best comedies, *Bullets Over Broadway,* for which he won another Best Screenplay Award in 1994.

Though he has created many hilarious films, Allen is a serious artist concerned with the fate of humankind. In 1986, Allen refused to allow his films to be shown in South Africa until that country ended its racist laws of apartheid. In 1990, along with fellow directors Martin Scorsese and Stanley Kubrick, he founded the Film Foundation, dedicated to preserving American films. Incredibly, many of Hollywood's historic movies have been lost, destroyed, or are turning to dust. Each year, the Film Foundation will restore and preserve several great films for future generations. Allen continues to live and work in New York City, attends many of the New York Knicks basketball games, and plays jazz clarinet every Tuesday night at a Manhattan nightclub.

Judy Blume

When Judy Blume was nearing the age of thirty, she realized she wanted to be a writer. She was a mother of two children and had a small business making felt banners to decorate children's bedrooms. But she worked hard at writing and became an influential and highly successful author.

Blume was born in Elizabeth, New Jersey. Her father was a dentist, and her mother was a housewife. Blume, then named Judy Sussman, enjoyed a stable family life.

When she entered New York University, her goals were to earn a degree in education and find a husband to take care of her. She hoped to live the same kind of life her mother had enjoyed. While at New York University, Blume met and married a lawyer with whom she had two children. She described her life as a wife and mother as "comfortable and uneventful. Somewhere along the way, my mother's wishes for me—a good husband and good provider—became my way of life. I didn't resent it. I only had second thoughts about it later."

Blume soon found herself composing children's stories in her head while she did the dishes each night. She wrote down the stories, illustrated them, and mailed her work to various publishers. Rejection after rejection arrived in the mail. Often, upon receiving a rejection letter, she hid in her closet so that her children would not see her and cried. "I worked myself up to the point where I could get six rejections a week. I would go to bed thinking, 'I'll never get anything published,' and wake up saying, 'I will too!'"

Soon, encouragement came from a new source. Blume enrolled in a writing class. For the class, she completed one chapter of a story each week. Her book, called *The One in the Middle is the Green Kangaroo*, was published in 1969. Never had Blume felt such pride in her own achievement.

Blume soon turned her attention to writing books for older children. She believed that there was not enough good writing for young adults that told the truth about life. Further, she knew that the teenage years were an exciting time in a person's life, and she wanted to write about them. "When you're twelve, you're on the brink of adulthood but everything is still in front of you and you still have the chance to be almost anyone you want. That seemed so appealing to me. I wasn't even thirty when I started writing, but already I didn't feel I had much chance myself."

Judy Blume indeed told young adults "the truth." Her novel *Are You There God? It's Me, Margaret* deals with the difficult topic of menstruation. *Iggie's House* is about racial prejudice. *It's Not the End of the World* tackles divorce and family breakups. *Deenie* discusses masturbation. *Blubber* portrays a socially ostracized girl. And *Forever...* addresses the feelings of first love. Before Judy Blume published these books, no author had spoken so frankly about the deeply emotional issues that most interest and confuse young adults. Her books helped countless young readers feel they are not alone in their thoughts and feelings. To this day, Judy Blume receives many letters from young adults thanking her for writing her books, or asking her advice.

Blume is not without her critics, however. Some parents think her books are too frank and too honest. Blume thinks these parents are misinterpreting what draws adolescents to her work. "What I worry about is that an awful lot of people . . . have gotten the idea that sex is why kids like my books. The impression I get from letter after letter is that a great many kids don't communicate with their parents. They feel alone in the world. Sometimes reading books that deal with other kids who feel the same things they do makes them feel less alone."

In order to address this problem of lack of communication between children and their parents, Blume established a special fund in 1981. Financed primarily with the royalties from a book she compiled titled *Letters to Judy: What Your Kids Wish They Could Tell You,* The Kids Fund gives $45,000 a year to organizations that help kids communicate with their parents.

Asked how it is that she came to be so perceptive about the feelings and experiences of young adulthood, Blume has said, "I have a capacity for total recall. That's my talent, if there's a talent involved. I have this gift, this memory, so it's easy to project myself back to certain stages in my life. And I write about what I know is true of kids going through those stages."

Judy Blume has won many children's literary awards. But she hopes that adults will read her work, too. She believes it can aid communication and understanding between parents and their children. She has no worries that her novels will become outdated or seem old-fashioned. "I think that my appeal has to do with feelings and with character identification. Things like that don't change from generation to generation."

Bob Dylan

SINGER AND SONGWRITER
1941–

Bob Dylan's nasal singing voice has been compared to the sound a cow makes when its leg is caught in a fence. But his vibrant music and his powerful, mysterious lyrics spoke for millions of America's young people during the 1960s.

Born Robert Zimmerman, Bob Dylan changed his name in honor of Irish poet Dylan Thomas. The Zimmerman family moved from Duluth to Hibbing, Minnesota, when Bob was six. Since he is fond of creating stories about his past, it is unclear exactly what sort of childhood Dylan had. During several interviews, he has talked of having run away from home. But many people who new Dylan as a boy remember his childhood in Hibbing as peaceful and happy. As a young man, Dylan dreamed of seeing the whole United States. Inspired by the folk music of Woody Guthrie, Dylan "hopped" freight trains and rode the rails with men who spent their lives traveling coast to coast as stowaways in boxcars. Like Guthrie, Dylan wanted to be a man of the people, to sing about the poor, and about the working-class men and women he admired.

In high school, Dylan took up the guitar and harmonica. When he was fourteen years old, he formed a band—The Golden Chords. The group was less than a hit, but Dylan did not give up his musical aspirations. Four years later, having enrolled in the University of Minnesota School of the Arts, Dylan performed in neighborhood coffee houses throughout Minneapolis and Saint Paul. During the 1960s, such places provided an informal atmosphere where singers and songwriters could perfect their craft. From 1959 until the end of the 1961 school year, Dylan played his guitar and harmonica and sang nearly every night. Mostly, he performed the songs of Woody Guthrie, who wrote "This Land is Your Land" and "So Long (It's Been Good to Know Ya)," among other famous tunes. Guthrie wrote most of his songs during the Great Depression. The songs often describe the struggles of people "down on their luck." Dylan wrote his own songs in the same spirit.

In 1961, when Dylan learned that Woody Guthrie was in a hospital in East Orange, New Jersey, he moved to New York City in hopes of meeting his hero. Guthrie agreed to meet the young folk singer and the two became friends. Guthrie encouraged Dylan to continue writing and singing his songs. Though he had no formal musical training, Dylan's performance improved with dedicated practice. He began to find his own way to deliver a song, with humor and emotional impact. Dylan's distinctive style projected power and conviction. Folk music fans soon took notice.

In April 1961, Dylan got his first big break. He was hired to open a concert for blues legend John Lee Hooker. A record executive in the audience that night signed Dylan to a recording contract. In record after record, Dylan sang out against the world's wrongs. Songs like "Masters of War," and "A Hard Rain's A Gonna Fall" warned those in power that a new generation of Americans would not accept things as they were. His song, "The Times They Are A Changin'" inspired countless young people and others to protest the Vietnam War, as well as racial discrimination and other social problems. Later, a violent revolutionary group called themselves The Weathermen after a Bob Dylan lyric that said: "You don't need a weatherman to tell which way the wind blows." The lyric might be interpreted as: "Don't trust people in power to tell you the truth."

By 1964, Bob Dylan was a hit folk artist playing 200 concerts a year. His fans loved his music and his rough singing style. But Dylan was always evolving as an artist. In 1965, he released a new album called *Bringing it all Back Home.* The album moved away from a folk sound toward rock and roll. Dylan had "gone electric" by using electric guitars, drums, and bass to give the songs even more power than his earlier work. Many fans who loved his old style were not convinced, however. At the 1965 Newport Folk Festival, Dylan and his new band were loudly booed.

Another artist might have been made nervous by such a reception, but Dylan never wanted his audience to become comfortable and bored with his music. In 1965, he released a historic album called *Highway 61 Revisited,* which contained his first huge hit "Like a Rolling Stone." Less than a year later, Dylan completed work on another landmark album of rock music, *Blonde on Blonde.*

On July 29, 1965, Dylan was nearly killed while riding his motorcycle at high speed. He broke his neck and also suffered a concussion, lacerations, amnesia, and partial paralysis. For nine months he lay in a hospital bed recovering. Fans feared for his life. But Dylan recovered, and in 1968 he released a quiet, self-searching album called *John Wesley Harding.*

In 1967, a documentary about Dylan titled *Don't Look Back,* was released. The film, which follows Dylan through a few typical days in his life, shows the pressures put upon a star of his magnitude. Everyone seems to want something from him. At one point he is asked by a journalist if anyone really "knows" him. "Nobody knows me," he replies. "Nobody knows you. Nobody really knows anyone." The movie reveals a smart, brooding, and often funny young man who seems very alone in the world.

Bob Dylan's incredible success and output continued into the early 1970s. It seems nearly impossible that one man could have created so much great music over so short a span of time. Dylan became a worldwide superstar and, like most rock musicians of the time, began to experiment with drugs. This experimentation contributed to his personal problems.

"Everything happened so quick in the sixties," he told the Los Angeles Times in 1984. "There was just electricity in the air. It's hard to explain. I mean you didn't want to go to sleep because you didn't want to miss anything. It wasn't there in the seventies and it ain't there now. If you want to really be an artist, you'll go and find the electricity. It's somewhere!"

In 1970, Princeton University presented Dylan with an honorary doctorate in music, the first ever awarded to an untrained musician. Throughout the 1970s, Dylan remained among the most popular musicians on earth. When it was announced that he and his band would tour the globe in 1974, an estimated 6 million ticket orders poured in. More than 650,000 people attended the 39 concerts.

Dylan's personal life was less successful. During these years, it seems clear that his lifestyle was taking a toll on his relationships and many friends began to turn away from him. In 1977, his wife divorced him and took their five children away from him.

Always one to surprise his fans, Dylan stunned the world in 1979 by announcing he had abandoned his Jewish roots to become a born-again Christian. The result was a number of great songs, among them "I Believe in You," "You're Gonna Serve Somebody," and "Slow Train Coming." Many of his fans disliked the new music simply because of its religious content. But others felt Dylan's music held renewed power and beauty. Always searching for answers, Dylan reportedly returned to Judaism in 1983. Though many thought his tour of Israel in 1987 was symbolic of this return to the Jewish faith, he dismissed the idea. "It's just another stop on the tour," he insisted.

In 1985, he participated in the recording of "We Are the World" along with most of rock and roll's greatest musicians. He also donated his time to Live Aid, a historic all-day concert that raised money to help victims of hunger, and he has made several appearances at the Farm Aid concerts that assist small farmers.

Dylan received the 1986 American Society of Composers, Authors, and Publishers Founders Award, which salutes musicians who changed popular music. In 1988 he was inducted into the Rock and Roll Hall of Fame in Cleveland, Ohio. When Bob Dylan turned fifty years old in 1991, many fans who had been young during the 1960s stopped to examine their own lives. It was hard for many to believe that the skinny folk singer who helped lead them in protest of the Vietnam War had become a middle-aged man. A huge group of the greatest rock and roll, folk, and country musicians gathered at New York's Madison Square Garden to perform Dylan's biggest hits. And as the tributes and awards continue to roll in, Bob Dylan continues to experiment, and continues to touch the minds and souls of his audience. New ablums in 1996 and 1997 marked a return to Dylan's blues roots. Just his guitar, harmonica, and time-worn but powerful voice create a strong, lonesome, and oddly beautiful sound.

Barbra Streisand

SINGER, ACTOR, DIRECTOR
1942–

Barbra Streisand's fans tend to be devoted to her with an almost religous fervor. Blessed with an incredible singing voice, an unconventional physical beauty, and magnetic charisma, Streisand has become a gifted actor, film director, and writer. Few individuals hold such power or command such respect.

Streisand was born in Brooklyn, New York, in 1942. Her father died just fifteen months after her birth. This led to a difficult childhood for Barbra. Her family was not exactly poor, but she remembers, "we didn't have anything." Her mother adhered strictly to Jewish laws and customs.

At age fourteen, Barbra saw the Broadway play *The Diary of Anne Frank,* which was based on the famous true story of a Jewish family who hid from the Nazis in an attic for several years during the Holocaust. The drama effected Streisand on many levels. First of all, she was terribly sad that Anne Frank, a teenager like herself, and the others were eventually discovered and murdered in concentration camps. Also, she was captivated by the play itself, the sense of magic that theater created. Finally, she loved the idea of performing, of moving an audience to tears. That afternoon, Barbra decided she wanted to be on the stage.

Her career in the theater began humbly. In her teens, she took a job as an usher in New York and then became a switchboard operator in a theater ticket office. But she had faith in herself: "I was certain I'd be famous one day. When I'd tell my mother about it she'd say, 'How can you be famous? You're too skinny.'" Streisand's mother recommended she learn secretarial skills instead of dreaming of acting. But Streisand would not listen. "I knew I had talent and I was afraid that if I learned how to type, I'd become a secretary." It is often those few who cannot bear to imagine another path who end up achieving their dreams. When Streisand was eighteen, she enjoyed her first big success. She won a talent show that opened the door to several singing jobs in New York nightclubs.

Every performer needs one big break to make it to the top. Barbra Streisand's big break came one night in 1962, when she was singing at the Blue Angel nightclub. David Merrick, a major producer of Broadway shows, happened to be in the audience. When he heard Streisand sing, he knew immediately that she was destined for greatness. He hired her to star as Miss Marmelstein in his latest Broadway show, *I Can Get it for You Wholesale.* Streisand was brilliant in the show. She was funny, sang magnificently, and helped to make the musical one of the big hits of the 1962 season.

The following year, Streisand released her first record album. *The Barbra Streisand Album* proved to be a hit, as did *The Second Barbra Streisand Album,* released some months later. Both became gold records—selling more than 250,000 copies. By the end of 1963, Streisand was one of the most popular singers in America, and with her appearances on television, she had already begun to develop a fanatical following.

In 1964, she starred in the Broadway show *Funny Girl,* based on the life and career of vaudeville and radio star Fanny Brice. The show was a smash, and Streisand—playing the lovable, daffy, but lonely Brice—fulfilled her role so effectively that many believed she was merely playing herself. The song "People," a beautiful ballad from the show, rose to number 5 on the *Billboard* music chart, and became Streisand's trademark song. In 1965, Streisand's television special *My Name is Barbra* won five Emmy awards. In 1967 when she gave a free concert in New York's Central Park, 150,000 fans jammed the grounds, and millions more watched on television. When the 1968 film version of *Funny Girl* was released, Streisand won a Best Actress Oscar for her performance. At the age of 26, Barbra Streisand had conquered Broadway, Hollywood, and the world. She had achieved a level of popularity matched only by such legends as The Beatles, Elvis Presley, and Frank Sinatra.

Into the 1970s, Barbra Streisand's success continued. Her leading roles in the film version of the Broadway musical *Hello Dolly!* and opposite Robert Redford in *The Way We Were* made those movies huge successes. In 1977, she won a Grammy Award and an Oscar for co-writing "Evergreen," the theme from her film *A Star is Born.*

During the late 1970s, Streisand began to appear in public less often. The years of concert tours had tired her out. In fact, she had developed terrible stage fright, and as she sang in public less frequently, each performance became a major event to her fans. But Streisand continued making movies, and she began to take a more powerful role behind the camera. In 1983, she wrote, produced, directed, and starred in *Yentl,* which was based on a book by the famous Jewish author Isaac Bashevis Singer. It told the story of a girl in nineteenth-century Orthodox Jewish community who had a passion for reading and learning. But since only boys were given an education, she posed as a boy so she could read the Jewish holy books with other students and rabbis.

Today, Barbra Streisand becomes involved only in films over which she holds total creative control. She both produced and directed *The Prince of Tides* (1991) and *The Mirror Has Two Faces* (1996). Critics have lashed out that her films are too much about Barbra and not enough about the story or characters. But Streisand's fans disagree. They love every frame of her movies and every note she sings.

Itzhak Perlman

VIOLINIST
1945 –

When Itzhak Perlman was only three years old he sat and listened attentively to a violin recital on Israeli radio. When the hour-long program ended he told his mother that he wanted to grow up to be a violinist. His mother soon bought him a toy violin, and within days he had learned to play tunes on it. Perlman grew up to become one of the greatest violinists in the world.

Itzhak Perlman was born in Tel Aviv, Israel, where his father, Chaim, was a barber. When Perlman was four years old he became seriously ill with polio and lost the use of his legs. Itzhak quickly adapted to his disability. Those who know Perlman say that wearing braces on his legs and using crutches has never much bothered him. His parents bought him a small secondhand fiddle for six dollars. Because he could no longer run and play, he concentrated on his music. Even at the age of five, he practiced relentlessly and he was soon admitted to the Tel Aviv Academy of Music. At ten years old, he performed his first solo recital. He played Rimsky-Korsakov's famous "Flight of the Bumblebee," a piece that demands great speed and precision.

In 1958, Perlman's life changed forever. Ed Sullivan, who hosted a popular TV variety show in the United States, traveled to Israel in search of new talent. Itzhak, now thirteen and considered a child prodigy in Israel, had given recitals on radio and in local concert halls. Sullivan was struck not only by the boy's incredible mastery of the violin, but by his courage and good humor in the face of his disability. Perlman appeared on *The Ed Sullivan Show* in February 1959 and was an immediate hit with American audiences. And Perlman loved the United States. He decided to stay and began training at the prestigious Juilliard School of Music in New York City.

In 1964, Perlman entered the Leventritt Competition. Winners are awarded $1,000 and, far more importantly, appearances with American symphony orchestras, including the world-famous New York Philharmonic. At age nineteen, Perlman was the youngest competitor to reach the finals, held in Carnegie Hall. Simply to play in Carnegie Hall was a great honor, and Perlman borrowed a 200-year old Guarneri violin from Juilliard's rare instrument collection for the occasion. Perlman won the competition, but in the ensuing celebration, the priceless Guarneri violin was stolen. "I was horrified," remembered Perlman. The instrument was discovered the next day for sale at a nearby pawnshop—for fifteen dollars!

Perlman's personal charm endeared him to the musicians at the New York Philharmonic. He and famous violinist Isaac Stern became fast

Itzhak Perlman in performance

friends. Stern not only liked Perlman's bad jokes and booming laugh, he believed the young man would one day be a truly great violinist. The audience for Perlman's New York Philharmonic debut agreed. He took five curtain calls as the crowd roared its approval. Following this success, and with

Stern's endorsement, Perlman toured the United States in 1965 and 1966 and then Europe in 1967. In the three decades that have followed, Itzhak Perlman has risen to the top of his profession. Today, many consider him the greatest living violinist.

There is a special quality to Perlman's playing, perhaps a reflection of his personality. His music is filled with life. When he played with the Israel National Youth Symphony in 1964, one critic wrote that Perlman "stole the show. His flow of pure sweet tone is unceasing. His bow arm is unfailingly strong and steady. . . . His fingering is dazzlingly swift and accurate. There is a joy and bounce to his playing that had old-timers . . . reaching back in their memories to the days of the youthful Heifetz to find a parallel." To be compared to Jascha Heifetz is high praise indeed.

In 1967, Perlman found the love of his life. He married a violinist named Toby Lynn Friedlander with whom he now has three children. Perlman has played all kinds of music as well as the classical. He has recorded a collection of Scott Joplin ragtime songs, as well as a collaboration with the great jazz pianist Oscar Peterson. In 1995, he even traveled to Poland to jam with some of the world's great klezmer musicians. Klezmer is a kind of rollicking jazz dance music favored by Eastern European Jews.

President Ronald Reagan often invited Perlman to the White House, and in 1986 presented him with the Medal of Freedom. President Reagan, a former actor, loved not only Perlman's music, but his wonderful smile and boisterous personality on stage. Perlman admits he has always loved attention: "Nothing bothers me . . . I'm never afraid of an audience. You have to be a little bit of a ham to enjoy the audience. And I do." Itzhak Perlman's recordings have sold millions of copies worldwide and he remains among the most recognizable faces in classical music.

Steven Spielberg

FILM DIRECTOR
1947–

When Steven Spielberg was five years old he saw a movie about the circus called *The Greatest Show on Earth*. He remembers his father reassuring him that the people on screen "can't get out at you." But, Spielberg later realized, "They *were* getting out at me. I guess ever since then I've wanted to try to involve the audience as much as I can, so they no longer think they're sitting in an audience."

Steven Spielberg was born in Cincinnati, Ohio, the eldest of four children. His father was an electrical engineer and computer technician who disciplined and pushed

Steven. Joseph McBride, author of a Spielberg biograhy, says that "Arnold [Steven's father] helped Steven learn to direct; he was the family story-teller; he was interested in science fiction. Steven is the combination of two remarkable parents." Steven's mother, a former concert pianist, indulged her son's wild imagination and encouraged him to have fun and enjoy life. The combination of discipline and creative drive helped create a movie-making genius.

The Spielberg family moved to Arizona when Steven was nine years old. As the only Jewish kid in the neighborhood, he was sometimes the subject of anti-Semitic remarks. He felt "different." In 1996, he admitted to inter-viewer Oprah Winfrey that he used to tape the end of his nose at night in a failed attempt to gradually make it appear "less Jewish." Overall, howev-er, Spielberg and his three younger sisters had a joyful childhood. As a boy, Spielberg took great pleasure in the kind of imaginative destruction that would later fill his movies. Once, he pulled the head off one of his sister's dolls and served it on a plate with lettuce and tomatoes. His sister Anne remembers, "When I was a baby they had to put chicken wire around the crib so he wouldn't throw toy cars at me."

When Steven discovered his father's 8-millimeter movie camera in the garage, his energies became more focused. His life as a movie director had begun. "Some kids get involved in a Little League team or in music, in band—or watching TV. I was always drowning in little home movies. That's all I did when I was growing up. That was my escape." Using his family and friends as actors, Spielberg produced many short films. In seventh grade, he made one called *Battle Squad.* His father got him permission to film some scenes in a real airplane, and Steven manipulated the camera bril-liantly to make it appear his friends were soaring upward, diving down, or spinning out of control in the parked plane. A year later, he won an award for a World War II movie he called *Escape to Nowhere.*

While still in high school, Spielberg wrote and directed his first feature-length film. *Firelight* was about an alien attack on the United States. Spielberg's parents paid for the film processing, and it was shown at a local theater. It was clear to Spielberg's parents that he had the talent and drive to succeed as a director and they did all they could to encourage his ambition.

After high school, Spielberg applied to—and was rejected by—all the prestigious film schools. Instead, he attended California State University at Long Beach and got a degree in English. But he never gave up his dream of becoming a film director. Film and television studios are not open to the general public. One must either work there or have permission to enter. But Spielberg did not let such restrictions get in his way. One day, he put on a suit and tie, grabbed his briefcase, and boarded a Universal Studios tour bus. "I remember getting off the bus," he said later. "We were all let off to go to the bathroom. Instead, I hid between two sound stages until the bus left and then I wandered around for three hours. I went back there every day for three months. I walked past the guard every day, waved to him, and he waved back. I always wore a suit and carried a briefcase . . . He assumed I was some kid related to some mogul and that was that."

In 1970, Spielberg got his first big break. On the basis of his twenty-two-minute film called *Amblin'*, Universal Studios hired Spielberg to direct television shows. Still only twenty-three, Spielberg was ecstatic. He directed episodes of a number of shows including *Columbo* and *Night Gallery*. His work was good enough that in 1971, he was allowed to direct *Duel*, a made-for-TV thriller about a traveling salesman terrorized by a semi-tractor truck. *Duel* is widely thought of today as the best movie ever made for television.

Duel's success led to many offers from motion picture studios. In 1974, Spielberg made his first feature movie, *Sugarland Express*, starring Goldie Hawn. It was a failure at the box office but Spielberg's obvious visual sense and strong story-telling earned him another chance. In 1975, Spielberg directed *Jaws,* a movie about a coastal town terrorized by a killer shark. Shooting the film was a tremendous challenge for Spielberg. Nearly all the action took place in the Atlantic Ocean, not an easy place to shoot a film. By every measure, the film was a success. Millions of terrified and thrilled moviegoers sank lower and lower in their seats with each attack of Spielberg's great white shark. *Jaws* began a whole new era in Hollywood. By piling up more than $400 million in box-office receipts, Spielberg had invented the "blockbuster."

Spielberg continued to perfect his invention. His biggest hits—*Close Encounters of the Third Kind* (1977), *Raiders of the Lost Ark* (1981), *E.T.: the Extra-Terrestrial* (1982), and *Jurassic Park* (1993)—are among the biggest hits of all time. *E.T.* was the highest-grossing film in history until it was topped by Spielberg's own *Jurassic Park.* Spielberg's movies often involve brilliant special effects. The artists creating such screen magic love to work with Spielberg because of his childlike enthusiasm. "He'll howl with glee if something is exciting to him—say a person getting attacked by a T. Rex. He just can't contain himself," said one technician.

But in addition to fantastic special-effects efforts, Spielberg has devoted his energies to more serious and thoughtful films. *The Color Purple* (1985) was a moving adaptation of Alice Walker's book about the struggles of a young African-American woman. *Empire of the Sun* (1987) was an epic, heart-rending World War II story about a British boy who was separated from his parents and survived on his own in a Japanese prison camp. *Amistad* (1997) told the story of a mutiny aboard an African slave ship and the legal battles that followed.

In 1993, Spielberg released his most important film to date, *Schindler's List.* The film is the true story of a non-Jewish German businessman named Oskar Schindler who risked his life and spent his personal fortune to save more than 1,000 Jews from being murdered by the Nazis during the

Holocaust. The movie contained graphic, realistic and horrible visions of Jews being tortured and murdered by Nazis, and as it was shot in black-and-white and ran nearly 3 ½ hours, critics feared that nobody would want to see it. On the contrary, audiences flocked to *Schindler's List,* and its release aroused a new wave of education about the Holocaust. Spielberg arranged free screenings of *Schindler's List* for high school students across the United States and donated all profits from the film to Jewish charities. He also established the Survivors of the Shoah Foundation (*shoah* means "holocaust" in Yiddish). The Shoa Foundation embarked on a unique project to record on videotape the stories of Holocaust survivors still living in the 1990s. This library of firsthand accounts will serve as a permanent resource to help ensure that future generations know about the Nazi's massive crime. The Shoah Foundation has also launched programs to document other massive human tragedies, such as the AIDS epidemic.

Schindler's List won the Academy Award for Best Picture, and after more than two decades of hard work and brilliant success, Spielberg was awarded an Oscar as Best Director. But awards such as these were not what Spielberg treasured. The thanks he received from Holocaust survivors, and the honor he felt at being allowed to tell their heroic stories meant more to him than anything he had experienced as a director.

On top of his reponsibilities as a director and producer, Spielberg has helped to found Dreamworks SKG with Jeffrey Katzenberg and David Geffen. The three Hollywood moguls hope to establish a huge Hollywood studio outside the traditional Hollywood system—a place where filmmakers can operate with more artistic freedom.

On top of all of this work, Spielberg is the devoted father of eight. He takes an active role as a parent, including telling endless bedtime stories. "Fathering is a major job," he says. "But I need both things in my life: my job as a director, and my kids to direct me."

Judith Resnik

Judith Resnik once said of herself and her fellow astronauts, "It doesn't enter any of our minds that we're doing something dangerous." In fact, by 1986, most Americans thought of shuttle missions as safe and routine. But on January 28, 1986, the world was reminded that launching a rocket-propelled ship into space is difficult and risky. Resnik and six other crew members died when the space shuttle *Challenger* burst into flames and exploded in the sky above the Kennedy Space Center in Florida. In some respects, the United States has still not recovered from this tragedy, more than a decade later.

As a crew member of the space shuttle *Discovery* in 1984, Judith Resnik had became the second woman to travel in outer space, and the first Jewish astronaut ever. (American Sally Ride had been the first woman in space in 1983.) But being labeled as "the first . . ." annoyed Resnik. She wanted to be known as, "just another astronaut, period." She added that, "Firsts are only the means to the end of full equality, not the end in itself." Henry Hartsfield, commander of Resnik's *Discovery* mission told a reporter that Resnik was, "an astronaut's astronaut. She was not satisfied with second-best." There were many ways in which Judith Resnik was not a typical astronaut. Until she was nearing thirty years old, she had little interest in space travel and no training as a pilot.

Resnik was born in Akron, Ohio. Her father was an optometrist and her mother was a radiologist. After years of fighting, the two divorced when Resnik was seventeen years old. Resnik maintained a close relationship with her father but lost contact with her mother following many bitter arguments. Her father said later that Resnik, "succeeded despite her family situation." Perhaps because of the troubles at home, Resnik became deeply involved at school. She was a serious student and the only female in the math club, another distinction she disliked. After the *Challenger* disaster, a high school classmate described Resnik for a reporter: "People had a lot of respect for her. She could be a lot of fun, but never silly." Even in high school, Resnik was an ambitious, well-organized perfectionist with little time to waste. She was the valedictorian of her class and received perfect scores on her college entrance exams.

At Carnegie Mellon University in Pittsburgh, Pennsylvania, Resnik became an engineering major and graduated among the top five students in the department. She married a fellow engineering student and both took jobs with the Radio Corporation of America. With money received as wed-

Judith Resnik (back row, far right) and the crew of the ill-fated space shuttle Challenger

ding gifts, they bought an upright Steinway piano. Resnik was musically gifted and might have pursued a career as a pianist had she not been so fascinated by mathematics and engineering.

While she worked for RCA, Resnik pursued a Ph.D. in engineering at the University of Maryland. During these years, she and her husband found themselves in a difficult situation. While her husband longed for children and a "normal" life, Resnik had no interest in raising a family. Though they loved and cared for one another, their dreams no longer were compatible.

They agreed to divorce in 1975, but remained best friends. After earning her Ph.D. in 1977, Resnik was unsure of what to do with her life. The idea of entering the U.S. space program captured her imagination. After all, what could be more challenging than being an astronaut? When friends noticed a National Aeronautics & Space Administration (NASA) application on her kitchen table, they thought it was a joke. Resnik had always been much more interested in math or looking into a microscope than shooting into outer space. Her father reasoned that she was "looking for a purpose in her life." Resnik wanted to "do something that really mattered."

Resnik eventually flew to Houston to take NASA's physical examination. Although she had been working out at a local gym and had been on a strict diet, she was worried she would not meet NASA's rigorous physical requirements. But a few days after the exam, at six a.m., she got a call saying that she and five others would be trained as the first female astronauts. She woke her father and all her friends to tell them the news. It was, she said later, the most exciting day of her life until she was being launched into space aboard the *Discovery.*

Judith Resnik's delicate face, dark eyes, and soft curls sometimes hid the fact that she was tough and opinionated. "She was headstrong," remembered Michael Coates, a fellow astronaut. "She always had to get her two bits in. But when she'd be all done arguing she'd just smile and that'd be it. You felt completely comfortable around her. In a lot of ways she was the ideal astronaut." In that terrible moment above the Kennedy Space Center in 1986, the United States lost seven remarkable people. One can only wonder what Judith Resnik might have gone on to do after retiring from the space program. As it is, she stands as testament to the idea that with a strong will and a deep commitment to excellence, a person can accomplish nearly anything.

Mark Spitz

OLYMPIC SWIMMER
1950 –

A combination of self-confidence and competitive drive helped make Mark Spitz the greatest American swimmer of all time. In the 1972 Olympic Games, he won seven gold medals and set four world records. In all, Spitz earned eleven medals during his Olympic career. Along with Spitz's mental approach, his body was perfect for the sport. Standing six feet one inch (185 centimeters) tall, Spitz was 170 pounds (77 kilograms) of solid muscle. Also, he had the curious ability to flex his legs slightly forward at the knee. This meant that each of his kicks drove deeper into the water and carried a bit of added power.

Spitz learned to swim in a YMCA swimming program in Sacramento, California. Even at age six, Spitz had the willingness to work hard to improve. He began swimming for an hour or more each day and quickly grew stronger and faster in the water than his friends: "I had no idea where I was going when I started swimming," he remembered years later. "It was more or less like a social activity with my friends, and I had goals to be someone like [football legend] Johnny Unitas." Soon, Spitz had become a serious swimmer. By the age of nine, he spent ninety minutes in the pool, four times a week. At age twelve, he got up at dawn and swam laps until it was time to go to school. After school, he headed for the pool and swam until dinner time.

Such drive to succeed convinced his father, a construction consultant, to take his son's potential seriously. Arnold Spitz moved his wife and three children to Santa Clara, California, so that fourteen-year-old Mark could work out at the Santa Clara Swim Club. The club was famous for producing top swimmers. Most importantly, Arthur Spitz wanted his son to work with respected Coach George Haines. In 1964, his first year under Haine's guidance, Spitz qualified for the national championships in the 400- and 1500-meter freestyle events, a fine showing. He met with less success the following year when he finished fifth and failed to qualify in the 1500-meter event at the American national championships.

Spitz regained his confidence when he took four gold medals and set four new records at the 1965 Maccabiah Games in Israel. Young Jewish athletes from around the world compete in the Maccabiah Games. Doing well against international competition helped Spitz believe he could succeed under pressure. Spitz faced pressure from himself and his father. Arnold Spitz was fond of asking his son: "How many lanes are there in the swimming pool?"

"Six!" Mark would answer.

"Right," Arthur Spitz would say. "And how many winners in a race?"

"One!" Mark would shout. In the Spitz household, second place was as good as finishing last.

In 1966, as a high school sophomore, Spitz won his first national title in the 100-meter butterfly. Then, in 1967, Mark Spitz had his first great year. He took four different national titles and set world records in the 100- and 200-meter butterfly events, and the 400-meter freestyle. At the Pan American Games in Winnipeg, Canada, he won five gold medals. *Swimming World* magazine named Spitz its "1967 World Swimmer of the Year." There seemed little doubt that Spitz would be among those chosen to represent the United States in the 1968 Olympic Games in Mexico City.

Spitz boldly announced he would take home six gold medals from the Mexico City Games. Such boasting did not sit well with his Olympic teammates and their resentment resulted in inexcusable name-calling. U.S. Coach Sherm Chavoor said, "They tried to run him off the team. It was 'Jew boy' this and 'Jew boy' that. It wasn't a kidding type of thing either. He didn't know how to handle it." This was Spitz's first real encounter with anti-Semitism. He blocked it out and trained hard. But at Mexico City, Spitz failed to win a single individual gold medal, though he did win a silver in the 100-meter butterfly and a bronze in the 100-meter freestyle. He also shared two gold medals in the team relay events. But Spitz's high standards did not allow him to see his performance as anything but a failure.

In 1969, Spitz was recruited to join the college's premier swimming team at Indiana University. He planned to swim competitively while studying to become a dentist. Spitz was eventually elected captain of the swim team and enjoyed a college career filled with NCAA titles and records. Indiana University won the national swimming title all four years Spitz was on the team. During his freshman year, Spitz was named Outstanding Athlete at the Maccabiah Games after collecting six gold medals. In 1971, Spitz was named the Amateur Athletic Union's James E. Sullivan Athlete of the Year. He was the first Jewish competitor to win that prestigious honor.

In 1972, Mark Spitz arrived at the greatest moment in his life and one of the most phenomenal performances in Olympic history. In Munich, Germany, he took the gold medal in all of the seven events in which he competed. In an eight-day exhibition of physical and mental perfection, Spitz won the 100- and 200-meter freestyle, the 100- and 200-meter butterfly, and three medals in team relay events. Not only did he win seven gold medals against the best swimmers the world had to offer, he set a new world record in each of the seven races. "Day in and day out, swimming is 90 percent physical," he told reporters. "You've got to do the physical work in training, and don't need much mental. But in a big meet like this, it's 90 percent mental and 10 percent physical. Your body is ready and now it becomes mind versus matter."

Tragically, the 1972 Olympics will always be remembered for a second reason. Palestinian terrorists kidnapped and murdered eleven Israeli athletes. Security agents worried that, as a Jew, Spitz might become another target and they hurried him away from the Olympic village.

Following the Olympics, it appeared as if Spitz would soon become a movie star. Several Hollywood studios were interested in casting him in films. He endorsed swimsuits and other products. But his intense, competitive personality made him ill suited for such work. He became impatient with the slow production process and argued with directors, producers, and corporate executives. In 1973, he married a former model and they had a son. Other than doing some occasional sports broadcasting, Spitz disappeared from the public eye. He was happy to coach his son's soccer team and enjoy his retirement from competitive sports.

Then, at age 40, Spitz attempted an incredible comeback. "I think we're going to redefine what forty-year-olds can do," he announced. With those words, Spitz began a battle to make the 1992 U.S. Olympic swim team and compete in Barcelona, Spain. Choosing to swim only in what was always his strongest event, the 100-meter butterfly, Spitz began a rigorous campaign to bring his body back to its 1972 form. At times, the old self-confidence bordering on arrogance showed itself: "I personally wouldn't want to swim against Mark Spitz in the Olympics," he told a group of reporters one day. It was not to be. Spitz was badly beaten in the Olympic trials and realized he had to give up his dream. He soon announced he was simply too old to compete against a new generation of great swimmers.

Mark Spitz was honored as "World Swimmer of the Year" in 1967, 1971, and 1972. Winner of a gaudy assortment of medals from the Olympic Games (nine gold, one silver, and one bronze,) the Pan American Games, Maccabiah Games, and his years competing in the NCAA, Mark Spitz remains the top swimmer the world has ever seen. Today's athletes are bigger and more powerful, so Spitz's world records have been broken. But no male swimmer has come close to matching his performance of 1972, or his glorious career.

Ben Cohen and Jerry Greenfield

FOUNDERS OF BEN & JERRY'S ICE CREAM
Ben (1951–)   Jerry (1951–)

Ben Cohen and Jerry Green-field were born in Brooklyn, New York, and attended the same grade school and high school. They became friends in seventh-grade gym class when each was too overweight and slow to be much good at track. In high school, the two rode around in Ben's convertible Camaro listening to music, and they remained friends even after going their separate ways following graduation.

As a senior in high school, Ben Cohen took a job as an ice

cream man. He moved up in the company to become responsible for distributing ice cream pops to all the ice cream men in his Brooklyn neighborhood. Cohen liked the job, and, following a year and a half at Colgate University, he resumed his duties. Later, he became interested in making pottery and jewelry and took any number of odd jobs to support himself. He worked as a cashier at McDonald's, mopped floors at a grocery store, and was a security guard at a racetrack.

In 1974, Cohen took a position as a crafts teacher working with emotionally disturbed adolescents. The Highland Community School was on a big plot of land in the Adirondack Mountains and included a working farm. Cohen enjoyed the school and believed the work was important. During his three years there, he built his own house and taught all sorts of courses in pottery, photography, filmmaking, and stained glass. Also, he began to make ice cream with his students.

In 1977, Cohen and his old friend Jerry Greenfield decided to go into business together. Greenfield had taken a somewhat more conventional approach to his career choices. After earning a national merit scholarship in high school, he had enrolled at Oberlin College. His dream was to become a doctor. But after college graduation, his medical school applications were all turned down. Still hoping to work in medicine, he took a job as a technician in a laboratory that was performing experiments on beef hearts. Grinding up beef hearts and looking at test tubes was not something Jerry enjoyed doing. After one year of boredom, he applied to medical school again, and was rejected.

It was a difficult time for Greenfield. He had to come up with a new dream in life. In 1974, he went to North Carolina with his wife-to-be and took another job as a lab technician. The job was not fulfilling, and it was an easy choice to go into business with his old buddy Ben Cohen.

Both men loved food, so there was no question they would go into the food business. At first, they wanted to make bagels, but they soon discovered that the ovens and machinery needed to start up such a business were too expensive. Ice cream was cheaper to make. So they began learning about ice cream. They started by signing up for a mail-order ice cream–making course. They completed the requirements and received a grade of "A." Both felt ready to start. The question was where to locate their business. They settled on Burlington, Vermont, because they liked the lively feeling of the college town—and because it had no ice cream parlor. This is often the way entrepreneurs work. They find a need and fill it. Cohen and Greenfield invested $8,000 of their own money and borrowed $4,000 more to start up Ben & Jerry's Ice Cream. They bought an old gas station and converted it into a store with ice-cream-making facilities. Perhaps most importantly, the two agreed on a "mission" for the new company. They hoped not only that the business would be profitable, but that the community would benefit from the way Ben & Jerry's did business.

Ben & Jerry's soon became known for its rich and unusual ice cream flavors as well as its strong commitment to improving people's lives. They also became famous for wacky promotional schemes. In 1986, Ben and Jerry's "Cowmobile" (a truck painted with black-and-white spots like a cow's) began touring the country passing out free samples. Outside Cleveland, however, the cowmobile caught fire and was completely destroyed. Undaunted, Greenfield and Cohen continued to promote fun within their company, even establishing a "Joy Gang" dedicated to making Ben & Jerry's a more playful place to work.

Still committed to their mission statement, Cohen and Greenfield believed in more than making good ice cream. As profits rose and the business grew strong, they established the Ben & Jerry Foundation to pass out small grants to individuals and groups dedicated to improving their local communities. Today, Ben & Jerry's Ice Cream gives away 7.5 percent of its annual earnings to worthy applicants.

The profits, of course, come from great products. Ben & Jerry's biggest hit was when they received permission from rock star Jerry Garcia to make an ice cream flavor named Cherry Garcia. A mix of maraschino cherries, chocolate chunks, and creamy vanilla ice cream, Cherry Garcia was a smash hit. Each new Ben & Jerry's product bears a funky name and is eagerly awaited by ice cream fans nationwide. Those concerned with gaining weight can now enjoy a line of low-fat frozen yogurt and sorbet.

Recently, Ben Cohen reflected on his pride in the company and his belief in its future. He believes Ben & Jerry's has great potential to grow and thrive "[not only because of] the quality of our product, but the way we do business, so that there's many people who buy our ice cream that believe in Ben & Jerry's, that believe in the company, believe in what we stand for."

Ben & Jerry's continues to be a model for any company hoping to make a profit while being a positive force for hopefulness in its community. That's one reason to buy Ben & Jerry's ice cream. Other reasons include Cherry Garcia, Chunky Monkey, New York Super Fudge Chunk, and Wavy Gravy. Ben & Jerry's Scoop Shops are open for business nationwide.

Jerry Seinfeld

COMEDIAN, ACTOR, WRITER
1954 –

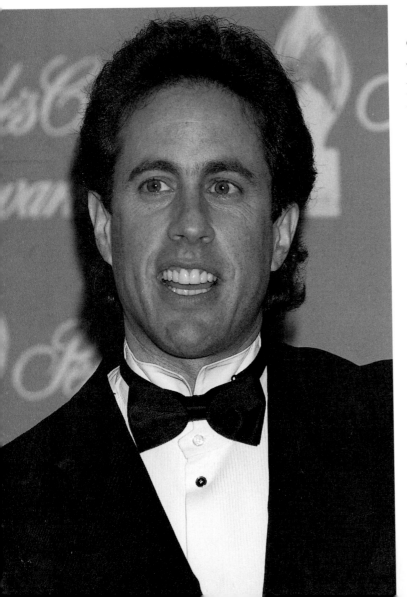

Jerry Seinfeld believes he was destined to make people laugh. "I knew I was going to be a comedian at a young age. I remember one time I made a friend laugh so hard that he sprayed a mouthful of cookies and milk all over me. And I liked it. That was the beginning." When he was eight years old, he saw a comedian on *The Ed Sullivan Show*. He did not understand exactly what the man was doing until his father explained: "This man's job is to come out and be funny for people." Jerry could not believe it: "'That's his whole job?' I asked. 'Are you kidding me?' And he said,

'No, he's kidding us!'"

Just like the man he saw on television, Seinfeld has made a career out of being funny. It's not as easy as it looks. A stand-up comedian is all alone on the stage and if the audience is not laughing it makes for a terrible night. Stand-up comedians travel from city to city staying alone in hotels and waiting to perform. Still, it's a life Jerry Seinfeld loves even more than working on his hugely successful *Seinfeld* television show.

Seinfeld grew up comfortably on Long Island, New York, wanting to be Superman, Spiderman, or Batman. Seeing that he would not be physically powerful enough to be a superhero, he concentrated on being funny. At thirteen, he taped interviews with his parakeet and made himself laugh. He was a loner, not very popular with other kids. "When you retreat from contact with other kids, your only playground left is your own mind. You start exploring your own ability to entertain yourself."

In 1976, on the night he graduated with honors from Queens College in New York City, he went to a nightclub called Catch A Rising Star. Here, young comedians waited in line all night for a chance to perform for a real audience. This time Seinfeld would not simply watch others, he would participate. When his name was called, Seinfeld took the stage and stood beneath a spotlight. It was the most terrifying moment of his life, and the most exhilarating. He loved being on stage all alone, with a chance to succeed or fail based purely on his own abilities. Most comedians fail miserably at first, and Seinfeld was no exception. He got few laughs, but made it through the ordeal. Despite many such failures, he never gave up his dream of becoming a stand-up comedian. His sister remembers he exhibited this sort of determination as a child: "He had a very ordinary childhood, but he was very driven. If he wanted a toy, he'd sit at the table arguing or crying or carrying on. He'd obsess about things like that. He still does, now that he's gotten to where he is."

During the next four years, Seinfeld worked tirelessly to perfect twenty-five minutes of material. Among his idols were famous comedians Robert Klein and Bill Cosby. Unfortunately for Seinfeld, making a living as a comedian is not an easy road. While he learned his craft, he took other jobs to support himself. He sold long-lasting lightbulbs over the phone. "This was a tough job," he says. "There aren't a whole lot of people sitting in the dark waiting for a phone call." Later he sold jewelry on the street and was often chased away by the police.

Finally, in 1981, he got his first big break. He was signed to perform on *The Tonight Show* hosted by Johnny Carson. This was the ultimate forum for a stand-up comic. In 1987 and 1988, Seinfeld got his own HBO specials. Today, he has appeared more than fifty times on *The Tonight Show* and *The David Letterman Show*.

In 1990, following various offers to appear in a situation comedy, he decided to write a show with his friend and colleague Larry David. David was a respected writer and comedian who had little success with audiences and did not like the life of a stand-up comic. The two decided their new show would be "a show about nothing." Seinfeld plays a character much like himself, surrounded by his selfish and quirky friends, all doing ordinary things. The genius of the show is that it centers around everyday events that are woven into an intricate story. Brilliantly written and performed, the show is very, very funny. The writers' key rules for the show's main characters are as follows: "No hugging, no learning." By 1991, the show had hit number one in the Nielsen ratings. In the past, a show about a Jew living in New York would probably not have been produced. Network executives often argued that such a show would not have "universal appeal." The huge success of *Seinfeld* led to other shows about Jewish characters, such as *Mad About You* and *The Nanny*.

Seinfeld admits he is still not really comfortable working on television.

"I'm the one who's dying because I can't act. I stink. I don't know what I'm doing." Whatever he is doing, he is doing it right, because the show remains among the most popular on television and is widely imitated. "We knew immediately it was a great show," he remembers. It will be interesting to see what project Seinfeld pursues following the inevitable end of his hit series. One thing is for sure, it will be comedy. "My whole life I was just trying to laugh—I'm obsessed with that moment," he has said. "When you're laughing, you've left your body, you've left the planet . . . It's an incredible experience."

124 Other Extraordinary Jewish Americans

Bella Abzug (1920–)
Three-term congresswoman from New York (1971–1977), known for her floppy hats, raspy voice, and biting wit. Ran unsuccessfully for the Senate, but continued her strong involvement in environmental protection and women's rights.

Cyrus Adler (1863–1940)
Scholar and Jewish-rights advocate. Taught at several major universities, then held positions at National Museum, Smithsonian Institution, and Jewish Theological Seminary. Protested anti-Semitic events in Russia, Poland, Palestine, and Germany.

Dankmar Adler (1844–1900)
German-born architect who settled in Chicago and was instrumental in creating many of the city's most notable buildings. Achievements include Central Music Hall, Auditorium Building, and a series of synagogues.

Madeleine Albright (1937–)
First woman appointed United States Secretary of State (1996), earlier served as U.S. representative to the United Nations. Raised as a Roman Catholic, discovered her Jewish heritage in her late fifties.

Isaac Asimov (1920–1992)
Russian-born scientist who published more than 300 books. Wrote science fiction, interpretations of Shakespeare, biblical studies, and numerous books on science for children and general reading.

Lauren Bacall (1924–)
Actress who achieved fame for her roles opposite Humphrey Bogart in films such

as *To Have and Have Not, The Big Sleep,* and *Key Largo.* Won Tony Awards for performances in the Broadway shows *Applause* (1970) and *Woman of the Year* (1981).

Bernard Baruch (1870–1965)
Wall Street tycoon who became an economic adviser to every U.S. president from Woodrow Wilson to John F. Kennedy.

Saul Bellow (1915–)
Author of numerous novels with philosophical themes, including *To Jerusalem and Back,* for which he won the Nobel Prize for Literature (1976). Also received the National Book Award three times—for *The Adventures of Augie March* (1953), *Herzog* (1965), and *Mr. Sammler's Planet* (1970).

Milton Berle (1908–)
Comedian and actor who became the first well-known television personality as the star of *The Texaco Star Theater* (1948–1953). Has received three Emmy Awards and has appeared in many movies and stage shows.

Carl Bernstein (1945–)
Washington Post investigative reporter who, with partner Bob Woodward, uncovered the Watergate cover-up that led to the resignation of President Richard Nixon. Later co-authored (with Woodward) *All the President's Men* (1974) and *The Final Days* (1976).

Barbara Boxer (1940–)
California congresswoman who has fought tirelessly for women's and children's rights as a U.S. representative (1984–1993) and as a U.S. senator since 1993.

Stephen Breyer (1938–)
U.S. Supreme Court justice appointed by President Bill Clinton in 1994 to succeed retiring justice Harry A. Blackmun.

James L. Brooks (1940–)
Writer, director, producer. Television credits include *Room 222, The Mary Tyler Moore Show, Lou Grant, Rhoda,* and *The Tracey Ullman Show.* Films include *Terms of Endearment, Broadcast News, Big,* and *The War of the Roses.*

Mel Brooks (1926–)
Comic writer, actor, and director whose most successful films include *The Producers* (1968), *Blazing Saddles* (1973), *Young Frankenstein* (1974), *Silent Movie* (1976), and *History of the World—Part I* (1981).

Lenny Bruce (1926–1966)
Stand-up comedian whose political humor and use of obscenity made him a counterculture hero of the 1960s. His stand on freedom of speech, despite many arrests, helped pave the way for the next generation of comedians.

Art Buchwald (1925–)
Syndicated newspaper columnist known for political satire. Books include *Son of the Great Society* (1966), *I Never Danced at the White House* (1973), *I Think I Don't Remember* (1987), and *Leaving Home: A Memoir* (1994).

Al Capp (1909–1979)
Cartoonist known for his comic strip "Li'l Abner," which ran in newspapers nationwide from 1934 until 1977. Later created "Fearless Fosdick," a parody of "Dick Tracy."

Benjamin Cardozo (1870–1938)
United States Supreme Court justice appointed by President Herbert Hoover. Served from 1932 until his death in 1938. Strong supporter of liberal social legislation.

Paddy Chayefsky (1923–1981)
Scriptwriter and dramatist best known for television play *Marty* (1953), which he adapted into an Oscar-winning film (1955). Also won Academy Awards for his screenplays of *The Hospital* (1971) and *Network* (1976).

Noam Chomsky (1928–)
Linguist concerned with the origin and nature of human language. Also an influential political thinker and activist known for his criticism of U.S. foreign policy.

Aaron Copland (1900–1990)
Leading American composer of the twentieth-century, created numerous operas, ballet scores, film scores, and concertos. Most famous for his ballets, including *Billy the Kid* (1938), *Rodeo* (1942), and *Appalachian Spring* (1944).

Howard Cosell (1918–1995)

Sportscaster and author known primarily for his play-by-play at boxing matches and, later, his commentary on *Monday Night Football* (1970–83).

Sammy Davis Jr. (1925–1990)

African-American singer, dancer, and actor who converted to Judaism as an adult. Best known for his performances in the films *Porgy and Bess* (1959), *Ocean's 11* (1960), *Robin and the 7 Hoods* (1964), and for the songs "What Kind of Fool Am I," "Candy Man," and "Mr. Bojangles."

Alan Dershowitz (1938–)

Defense attorney and law professor specializing in constitutional rights. A strong and outspoken advocate of free speech, most famous for winning the appeal that overturned Claus von Bulow's murder conviction.

E.L. Doctorow (1931–)

Novelist known for mixing fact with fiction. Famous works include *The Book of Daniel* (1971), *Ragtime* (1975), *World's Fair* (1985), and *Billy Bathgate* (1989).

Kirk Douglas (1918–)

Actor and director, best known for his portrayals of tough-but-decent men. Films include *Paths of Glory* (1957), *Spartacus* (1960), *Lonely Are the Brave* (1962), *The Fury* (1978), *The Man from Snowy River* (1982), *Greedy* (1994), and about fifty others.

Michael Douglas (1944–)

Son of Kirk Douglas and movie star known for playing the leading man in action-adventure and comedy. Films include *Romancing the Stone* (1984), *Jewel of the Nile* (1985), *Fatal Attraction* (1987), and *The War of the Roses* (1989). Also a movie producer who brought the highly acclaimed *One Flew Over the Cuckoo's Nest* to the screen in 1975.

David Dubinsky (1892–1982)

President of International Ladies' Garment Workers' Union (ILGWU) from 1932 to 1966. Vice president of American Federation of Labor (1934). Helped found American Labor Party (1936), Liberal Party (1944), Americans for Democratic Action (1947), and International Confederation of Free Trade Unions (1949).

Michael Eisner (1942–)
After taking over as chairman of the Walt Disney Company in 1984, Eisner has become one of the most influential people in the media industry.

Nora Ephron (1941–)
Novelist, screenwriter, and director whose credits include *When Harry Met Sally . . .* (1989), *Sleepless in Seattle* (1993), and *Michael* (1996).

Abe Fortas (1910–1982)
Supreme Court justice appointed by President Lyndon Johnson in 1965. Helped establish the rights of poor people to legal counsel.

Helen Frankenthaler (1928–)
A pioneer in the style of abstract art called color-field painting. Known for producing large paintings. For example, *Guiding Red* (1967), measures (30 x 16 feet) (9 x 4.9 meters).

Felix Frankfurter (1882–1965)
Supreme Court justice appointed by President Franklin D. Roosevelt in 1939. Considered a liberal and a Zionist, he helped found the American Civil Liberties Union in 1920.

Milton Friedman (1912–)
Economist whose conservative, free-enterprise-based theories have had a powerful impact on U.S. policy. Won Nobel Prize for Economics in 1976.

Casimir Funk (1884–1967)
Biochemist who pioneered the study of vitamins. First to isolate substance known as Vitamin B-1, or thiamine. Contributed to an understanding of vitamin deficiency.

Allen Ginsberg (1926–1997)
Poet and leading member of the Beat Generation. Works included the long poem "Howl" as well as *Reality Sandwiches* (1963) and *Planet News* (1969). Contributed to greater freedom of expression among writers and artists.

Arthur Goldberg (1908–1990)
Secretary of labor under President John F. Kennedy, then appointed to Supreme Court in 1962. Served as U.S. ambassador to United Nations (1965–68).

Rube Goldberg (1883–1970)

Cartoonist known for elaborate drawings of complex fantasy contraptions designed to perform simple tasks. Won Pulitzer Prize for editorial cartooning in 1948.

Emma Goldman (1869–1940)

Anarchist who rose to fame by protesting for workers' rights in the early 1900s.

Barry Goldwater (1909–)

Conservative U.S. senator from Arizona, served in Congress from 1952 to 1987. Ran unsuccessfully as Republican candidate for president in 1964.

Rebecca Gratz (1781–1860)

Founder of Female Hebrew Benevolent Society in 1819, first Jewish charity in the United States. Was in love with a gentile, but chose lifelong spinsterhood rather than marry outside her Jewish faith.

Alan Greenspan (1926–)

Influential economist, appointed by President Ronald Reagan to be chairman of the Federal Reserve Board in 1987; retained in that post by Presidents George Bush and Bill Clinton.

Ben Hecht (1894–1964)

Journalist, novelist, and playwright known for his stories of big-city life. Works include *Erik Dorn* (1921), *The Collected Stories of Ben Hecht* (1945), *The Front Page* (1928), and *20th Century* (1932). Also an active Zionist.

Sidney Hillman (1887–1946)

Labor leader, president of the Amalgamated Clothing Workers of America for thirty years, and a founder and first vice president (1935–40) of the Congress of Industrial Organizations (CIO).

Abbie Hoffman (1936–1989)

Radical leader of the 1960s, famous as one of the "Chicago Seven," accused of inciting anti-Vietnam War riots at 1968 Democratic National Convention.

Dustin Hoffman (1937–)
Stage and screen actor known for his versatility. Began movie career in *The Graduate* (1967). Other works include *Midnight Cowboy* (1969), *Papillon* (1973), *Lenny* (1974), *All the President's Men* (1976), *Kramer vs. Kramer* (1979), *Tootsie* (1982), *Death of a Salesman* (1985), and *Rain Man* (1988).

Nat Holman (1896–1995)
Legendary basketball player and coach. Member of the Original Celtics. Known as one of the game's great passers and was among the first in the history of basketball to sign individual contracts. Later went on to play for the New York Hakoahs, an all-Jewish team. Coached the only team to win both NCAA and NIT titles in the same year (1950).

Vladimir Horowitz (1904–1989)
Piano virtuoso who achieved worldwide fame over six decades. Escaped from Soviet Union in 1925 and, after years of living in America, returned to Moscow for a series of historic performances in 1986 at age eighty-two.

Louis Kahn (1901–1974)
Major architect of the twentieth century. Designed Yale University Art Gallery, Salk Institute for Biological Studies, library at Phillips Exeter Academy, Kimbell Art Museum, and Yale Center for British Art.

Danny Kaye (1913–1987)
Stage, film, and television comedian. Starred in *The Court Jester* (1956), *The Five Pennies* (1959), *The Secret Life of Walter Mitty* (1947), and *Hans Christian Andersen* (1952). Received two honorary Oscars.

Jerome Kern (1885–1945)
Composer for American musical theater. Works include *Show Boat* (1927), *Music in the Air* (1932), and *Roberta* (1933). Received Oscars for songs "The Way You Look Tonight" and "The Last Time I Saw Paris." Other songs include "Ol' Man River," "Smoke Gets in Your Eyes," and "All the Things You Are."

Calvin Klein (1942–)
Top American fashion and fragrance designer. Named "designer of the year" in 1993 by the Council of Fashion Designers of America for both his menswear and

women's wear. One of the first fashion designers to create designer jeans in the late 1970s.

Edward Koch (1924–)
Popular three-term mayor (1978–90) of New York City. U.S. Representative from New York (1969–77). Author of *Mayor* (1984) and *Politics* (1985), *His Eminence and Hizzoner* (1989), and *Citizen Koch* (1992). In 1997, took on the role as the judge on the television show *The People's Court.*

Ted Koppel (1940–)
Television newsman most famous as host of *Nightline.* Previously worked as radio and television news anchor.

William Kuntsler (1919–1995)
Lawyer best known for his defense of the "Chicago Seven" in 1969. Also defended American Indian militants in Wounded Knee case (1974) and convicts involved in Attica Prison Riot trial (1975).

Ralph Lauren (1930–)
Internationally renowned fashion designer with lines of men's, women's, and children's clothing, fragrances, shoes, jewelry, luggage, linens, furniture, and even paint. Empire includes more than 100 Polo/Ralph Lauren stores around the world. Active in many charitable causes, especially the fight against breast cancer.

Norman Lear (1922–)
Television and film writer, producer, and director most famous for landmark situation comedy *All in the Family* (debut, 1971). Other series include *Maude* (1972), *Sanford and Son* (1972), and *The Jeffersons* (1975). Founded liberal organization People for the American Way (1980).

Issac Leeser (1806–1868)
First rabbi in America to deliver sermons in English. Helped develop schools for Jewish children, and Jewish hospital, Jewish orphanage, and foster home for Jewish children. Founded the Jewish Publication Society (1845) and printed books in Hebrew.

Herbert H. Lehman (1878–1963)
Prominent figure whose career in public service included terms as a U.S. senator, New York governor, and director of the United Nations Relief and Rehabilitation project.

Benny Leonard (1896–1947)
Lightweight boxing champion from 1917 to 1925. Considered by many to be the best boxer of all time.

Barry Levinson (1942–)
Filmmaker, director, and screenwriter known for *Diner* (1982), *The Natural* (1984), *Tin Men* (1987), *Good Morning, Vietnam* (1987), *Rain Man* (1988), *Avalon* (1990), *Bugsy* (1991), *Sleepers* (1996), and *Donnie Brasco* (1997).

Nancy Lieberman-Cline (1958–)
Women's college basketball star of the late 1970s; one of the most prominent female athletes of her time.

Walter Lippmann (1889–1974)
Syndicated newspaper columnist and editor who focused on politics, economics, and philosophy. Founded *New Republic* in 1914. Editorial page editor of New York *World* (1929–1931). Later wrote for New York *Herald Tribune*. Won Pulitzer Prizes in journalism (1958 and 1962).

Julia Louis-Dreyfus (1961–)
Actress whose first prominent role was as a regular on *Saturday Night Live* from 1982 to 1985. From 1990 to 1998, starred as Elaine on the hit series *Seinfeld,* a role that won her both an Emmy Award and a Golden Globe Award.

Norman Mailer (1923–)
Journalist and novelist known for his brash, tough views on social and political issues. Books include *The Naked and the Dead* (1948), *An American Dream* (1965), *Miami and Siege of Chicago* (1969), *The Executioner's Song* (1979), and *Oswald's Tale* (1995).

Bernard Malamud (1914–1986)
Novelist known for his stories of Jewish life in America. Works include *The Natural* (1952), *The Assistant* (1957), and *The Fixer* (1966), for which he won the Pulitzer Prize.

Louis Marshall (1856–1929)
Prominent lawyer and statesman; strong advocate for Jews worldwide; helped establish Jewish Theological Seminary.

Adah Issacs Menken (1835–1868)
Actress and poet most famous for her role of Mazeppa (1863) in a play based on Byron's poem, during which she was tied, almost naked, to the back of a horse that galloped across the stage.

Bette Midler (1945–)
Singer/actress known as "The Divine Miss M." Films include *The Rose* (1979), *Divine Madness* (1980), *Ruthless People* (1986), *Outrageous Fortune* (1987), *Big Business* (1988), *Beaches* (1988), and *The First Wives Club* (1996).

Marvin Miller (1917–)
Economist, labor lawyer, and executive director of the Major League Baseball Players Association during the 1970s and 1980s. Helped bring about free agency, pension benefits, and today's huge salaries.

Vince Neil (1961–)
Born Vince Neil Wharton. Singer and songwriter best known for his work with rock groups including Mötley Crüe. In 1993 released a platinum-selling solo album, *Exposed*.

Paul Newman (1925–)
Film actor most famous for *The Hustler* (1961), *Cool Hand Luke* (1967), *Butch Cassidy and the Sundance Kid* (1969), *The Sting* (1973), *Absence of Malice* (1981), *The Verdict* (1982), *Mr. and Mrs. Bridge* (1990), and *Nobody's Fool* (1994). His "Newman's Own" line of food products donates profits to charity.

Adolph Ochs (1858–1935)
Purchased the *New York Times* in 1896 and turned it into one of the most influential and respected newspapers in the world.

Clifford Odets (1906–1963)
Playwright known for dramas centered around social injustice. Best known for *Awake and Sing!* (1935), *Golden Boy* (1937), *The Country Girl* (1950), and *The Flowering Peach* (1954).

Robert Oppenheimer (1904–1967)
Physicist who directed the development of the atomic bomb ("The Manhattan Project") during World War II. Recipient of Atomic Energy Commission's prestigious Fermi Award.

Grace Paley (1922–)
Fiction writer whose short stories center around New Yorkers and their relationships. Works include *The Little Disturbances of Man* (1959), *Enormous Changes at the Last Minute* (1974), *Later, the Same Day* (1985), and *The Collected Stories* (1994).

William S. Paley (1901–1990)
Founder of the Columbia Broadcasting System (CBS). Purchased a small network of radio stations in 1928 and built it into what is now CBS, one of the four major television networks in the nation.

Dorothy Parker (1893–1967)
Writer, poet, and critic, known for her biting wit and her short–story collections. Most notable was *After Such Pleasures* (1933), which featured her most famous story, *Big Blonde.* Also wrote film scripts and plays.

S. J. Perelman (1904–1979)
Humorist, playwright, and screenwriter. Work appeared regularly in *The New Yorker* magazine. Most well-known Broadway play was *One Touch of Venus* (1943).

Joseph Pulitzer (1847–1911)
Newspaper publisher, responsible for success of *St. Louis Post-Dispatch* and *The New York World.* Left large sums of money to Columbia University School of Journalism and established the Pulitzer Prize.

Ayn Rand (1905–1982)
Writer who came to America from Russia and originated a philosophy called Objectivism, which emphasizes the individual's rights in a capitalist society. Dramatized her philosophy in several well-known novels, including *The Fountainhead* (1943) and *Atlas Shrugged* (1957).

Man Ray (1890–1976)
Photographer, painter, sculptor. One of the founders of the New York City Dada movement. Experimented with various photographic techniques. Also made several surrealist films.

Jerry Reinsdorf (1936–)
Successful businessman who has become one of the most influential men in professional sports through his ownership of the Chicago Bulls and Chicago White Sox.

Buddy Rich (1917–1987)
Jazz drummer known for his amazing speed and skill. Performed in vaudeville at age two. Joined Tommy Dorsey's band in 1939. Formed his own big band in 1966.

Julius Rosenwald (1862–1932)
Philanthropist, served as president of Sears, Roebuck & Company (1910–1925), then became chairman of the board. Julius Rosenwald Fund has contributed millions of dollars toward the education of African-Americans and Jews.

David Lee Roth (1954–)
Rock star who rose to fame as lead singer for the group Van Halen. Later went on to produce numerous solo albums including *Crazy From the Heat* (1984), *Skyscraper* (1988), *A Little Ain't Enough* (1991) and *Dave's Greatest Hits: The Best* (1997).

Philip Roth (1933–)
Fiction writer whose work centers on Jewish life in America. Most famous works include *Goodbye, Columbus* (1959), *Portnoy's Complaint* (1969), *The Ghost Writer* (1979), *Zuckerman Unbound* (1981), *The Anatomy Lesson* (1983), and *The Counterlife* (1986).

Mark Rothko (1903–1970)
Painter in the abstract expressionist style whose most famous works consist of brightly colored rectangles against a vivid field.

Helena Rubenstein (1870–1965)
Polish American beauty expert, cosmetics manufacturer, author, and philanthropist. Owned factories on five continents, employing more than thirty thousand people. Known as one of the world's most successful businesswomen.

Arthur Rubinstein (1887–1982)
Classical pianist who toured the world, playing both as soloist and with major symphony orchestras. Enjoyed a long career that began when he was seven.

Winona Ryder (1971–)
Actress whose film credits include *Beetlejuice* (1988), *Edward Scissorhands* (1990), *Age of Innocence* (1993), *Reality Bites* (1994), *Little Women* (1994), and *The Crucible* (1996).

Carl Sagan (1934–1997)
Scientist and author whose writing and television shows helped millions understand science. Professor of astronomy at Cornell (1968–97). Participated in the space program and spoke out against nuclear war. Books include *The Dragons of Eden* (1977), *Broca's Brain* (1979); *Cosmos* (1980), and *Pale Blue Dot* (1995). Just before his death, served as co-producer for the film *Contact* (1997), which was based on his novel.

Adam Sandler (1966–)
Comedian who rose to fame on *Saturday Night Live* and has starred in several movies. Well known for "The Chanukah Song," a staple of his stand-up comedy routine.

David Sarnoff (1891–1971)
Giant of the radio and television industries who built the NBC network.

Adolph Schayes (1928–)
High-scoring forward who helped the Syracuse Nationals become one of NBA's top teams in the 1950s. A 12-time All-Star; scored 19,249 points and set a record with 1,059 games played. Later coached Philadelphia and Buffalo and served as an NBA supervisor of officials. Inducted into the Basketball Hall of Fame (1972).

Jacob Schiff (1847–1920)
Financier who backed many important railroads. Also very involved in large industrial companies, as well as the affairs of foreign countries. Established Harvard's Semitic Museum and was a founder of American Jewish Committee.

Menachem Mendel Schneerson (1902–1994)
Grand rabbi of Lubavitcher Hasidim, a sect of Orthodox Judaism. Based in Brooklyn, New York, Schneerson reached out to Jews all over the world, urging them to return to more traditional practices. Believed by many of his followers to be the Messiah.

Allan "Bud" Selig (1934–)
Co-owner and president of the Milwaukee Brewers baseball team since 1970. In 1991, became Major League Baseball's interim commissioner and commanded the sport during the turbulent labor negotiations of the mid-1990s.

Ben Shahn (1898–1969)
Painter and lithographer known for realistic works inspired by social and political events. Later became interested in murals and photography. Eventually work became more abstract.

Jerry Siegel (1914–1996)
Cartoonist who co-created the "Superman" comic strip in 1934. Four years later, Siegel and his partner sold off the rights to the strip to DC Comics for $130 in cash, thus signing away their share of the more than $1 billion that the Superman character would generate over the years.

Abba Hillel Silver (1893–1963)
Led the Zionist movement to a more politically active role in securing the establishment of a Jewish state in Palestine. Chairman of the American Section of the Jewish Agency (1946–1948). Reform rabbi of the temple in Cleveland, Ohio.

Neil Simon (1927–)
Playwright whose many Broadway hits include *Come Blow Your Horn* (1961), *Barefoot in the Park* (1963), *The Odd Couple* (1965), *Plaza Suite* (1968), *The Sunshine Boys* (1972), *Brighton Beach Memoirs* (1983), *Biloxi Blues* (1985), *Broadway Bound* (1986), and *Lost in Yonkers* (1991). Many of his plays have been adapted as successful movies.

Paul Simon (1941–)
Singer/songwriter whose partnership with Art Garfunkel was one of the most successful in popular music history. Among their albums: *Sound of Silence* (1966), *Parsley, Sage, Rosemary, and Thyme* (1966), *The Graduate* (1968), and *Bridge Over Troubled Water* (1970). Simon's solo albums include *There Goes Rhymin' Simon* (1973), *Still Crazy After All These Years* (1977), and *Graceland* (1985).

Isaac Bashevis Singer (1904–1991)
Novelist and short-story writer whose works usually depicted the lives of Jews in Eastern Europe, his homeland before coming to the United States. His epic trilogy consists of *The Family Moskat* (1950), *The Manor* (1967), and *The Estate* (1970). Other works include *Love and Exile* (1984) and *Enemies: A Love Story* (1987). Won the Nobel Prize for Literature in 1978.

Stephen Sondheim (1930–)
Broadway composer and lyricist whose lyrics for *West Side Story* (1957) won him critical acclaim. Other credits include *A Funny Thing Happened on the Way to the Forum* (1962), *A Little Night Music* (1973), *Sweeney Todd* (1979), *Sunday in the Park with George* (1984), *Into the Woods* (1987), and the film *Dick Tracy* (1990).

Susan Sontag (1933–)
Author and social critic whose works include *The Benefactor* (1963), *Death Kit* (1967), *I, Etcetera* (1978), *Styles of Radical Will* (1969), *On Photography* (1977), *Illness as Metaphor* (1978), *Under the Sign of Saturn* (1980), and *AIDS and Its Metaphors* (1989).

George Soros (1930–)
Immigrant from Eastern Europe who amassed a multi-billion-dollar fortune in the stock market and is now a currency speculator.

David Hackett Souter (1939–)
United States jurist and U.S. Supreme Court justice (1990).

Arlen Specter (1930–)
Republican senator from Pennsylvania. Lawyer and district attorney in Philadelphia, first elected to the Senate in 1980. Reelected in 1986 and 1992. Ran unsuccessfully for president in 1996.

Art Spiegelman (1941–)
Cartoonist and author who won a Pulitzer Prize for his controversial graphic novel *Maus: A Survivor's Tale.* The book is a comic book version of his family's experiences in the Holocaust. In it Jews are portrayed as mice and Nazis as cats.

George Steinbrenner (1930–)
Controversial principal owner of the New York Yankees and chairman of the board of the American Ship Building Company.

David Stern (1942–)
Commissioner of the National Basketball Association (NBA) who has been credited with devising a marketing scheme that has made the NBA one of the most popular sports entities in the world.

Howard Stern (1954–)

Radio disk jockey whose controversial on-the-air comments have won him much criticism, many fines, and millions of listeners. His autobiography, *Private Parts* (1993), was a best-seller, later made into a hit movie (1996).

Isaac Stern (1920–)

Violinist who picked up the instrument at a very young age and went on to become one of the greatest players in the world. Equally comfortable with classical and contemporary works, he has contributed sound tracks for numerous films, including *Fiddler on the Roof* (1971). A documentary of his 1979 tour of China *(From Mao to Mozart: Isaac Stern in China)* won an Academy Award in 1982.

Lee Strasberg (1901–1982)

Actor, director, and drama teacher, influenced hundreds of actors with "the Method." Co-founded (1931) the Group Theatre. Artistic director of Actors Studio (1948–1982). Trained Marlon Brando, Paul Newman, and many others.

Henrietta Szold (1860–1945)

Founder and first president of Hadassah, women's Zionist organization. A co-founder of the Jewish Publication Society of America, and editor of *American Jewish Yearbook* (1892–1916) and *Jewish Encyclopedia*. Worked to establish harmony between Jews and Arabs. Helped rescue Jewish children from Holocaust through Youth Aliyah.

Edward Teller (1908–)

Physicist who made major contribution to development of nuclear weapons. Worked on the Manhattan Project during World War II and also produced much of the theory behind the hydrogen bomb.

Sophie Abuza Tucker (1884–1966)

Famed vaudeville performer known as the "Last of the Red-Hot Mamas."

Steven Tyler (1948–)

Rock star who is the lead singer for the group Aerosmith. Father of film actress Liv Tyler.

Leon Uris (1924–)
Novelist and screenwriter known for placing fictional protagonists in historical situations. Books include *Exodus* (1959), *Armageddon* (1964), *Topaz* (1967), and *QB VII* (1970). Original screenplays include *Gunfight at the OK Corral* (1957).

Eddie Vedder (1964–)
Born Edward Louis Seversen III. Musician, singer, songwriter who founded the band Pearl Jam. The band's first album, *Teri,* became one of the biggest hits of 1991. In 1993, the band won a Grammy Award for Best Hard Rock Performance.

Mike Wallace (1918–)
Broadcast journalist known for his relentless interview style, especially as a correspondent on television's *60 Minutes* (1968–). Also author of several books, including *Mike Wallace Asks* (1958) and *Close Encounters* (1984).

Walter Winchell (1897–1972)
Syndicated newspaper columnist who created the modern gossip column. Adapted the format for radio in 1932 and gathered an audience of twenty million listeners. Best known for his column, "On Broadway," in the New York *Daily Mirror.*

Herman Wouk (1915–)
Novelist whose work centers around conflicts created by traditional values. Best-known books include *The Caine Mutiny* (1951), *Marjorie Morningstar* (1955), *The Winds of War* (1971), and *War and Remembrance* (1978). Won Pulitzer Prize for fiction in 1952.

For Further Information

For Younger Readers (ages 10–14)

Anderson, Kelly. *Immigration.* Lucent Bks., 1993.

Berg, Julie. *Maurice Sendak.* Abdo & Daughters, 1993.

Blume, Judy. *Are You There God? It's Me, Margaret.* Simon & Schuster, 1991.

Blume, Judy. *Judy Blume & You, Friends For Life.* Dell, 1991.

Borland, Kathryn K. and Helen R. Speicher. *Harry Houdini: The Young Magician.* Simon & Schuster, 1991.

Brooks, Philip. *The United States Holocaust Memorial Museum.* Children's Press, 1996.

Burton, Humphrey. *Leonard Bernstein.* Doubleday, 1994.

Butwin, Frances. *Jews of America: History & Sources.* Behrman, 1995.

Collins, Tom. *Steven Spielberg: Creator of E.T.* Silver Burdett, 1983.

Epstein, Rachel. *Anne Frank.* Franklin Watts, 1997.

Fisher, Leonard E. *Ellis Island: Gateway to the New World.* Holiday, 1986.

Freedman, Suzanne. *Louis Brandeis:The People's Justice.* Enslow, 1996.

Gay, Kathlyn and Martin. *Emma Goldman.* Lucent, 1996.

Glassman, Bruce S. *Arthur Miller.* Silver Burdett, 1990.

Goldish, Meish. *Levi Strauss.* Rourke, 1993.

Goodman, Michael E. *Boston Celtics.* Creative, 1993. (Relating to **Red Auerbach**)

Henry, Christopher. *Ruth Bader Ginsburg.* Franklin Watts, 1994.

Henry, Sondra and Emily Taitz. *Betty Friedan: Fighter for Women's Rights.* Enslow, 1990.

Hoffman, Joseph. *Jews in Sports.* Pitspopany, 1996.

Hurwitz, Joanna. *Leonard Bernstein: A Passion for Music.* JPS, 1993.

McPartland, Scott. *Edwin Land.* Rourke, 1993.

Meachum, Virginia. *Steven Spielberg: Hollywood Filmmaker.* Enslow, 1996.

Milgrim, Shirley. *Haym Salomon: Liberty's Son.* JPS, 1975.

Older, Jules. *Ben & Jerry's . . . The Real Scoop!* Chapters Pub., 1993.

Philips, Angela. *Discrimination.* Simon & Schuster, 1993.

Resnick, Abraham. *Holocaust.* Lucent, 1991.

Sanford, William R. and Carl R. Green. *Sandy Koufax.* Silver Burdett, 1993.

Sendak, Maurice. *Where the Wild Things Are.* Jantillana, 1995.

Sherrow, Victoria. *Jonas Salk: Research for a Healthier World.* Facts on File, 1993.

Spiegelman, Art. *Maus: A Survivor's Tale (Volumes I & II).* Pantheon, 1991.

Stafford, Mark. *W. E. B. Dubois: Scholar & Activist.* Chelsea House, 1989.

Stern, Ellen N. *Elie Wiesel: A Voice for Humanity.* JPS, 1996.

Stoppleman, Monica. *Jewish.* Children's Press, 1996.

Tyson, Peter. *Groucho Marx.* Chelsea House, 1995.

Venezia, Mike. *George Gershwin.* Children's Press, 1994.

Woog, Adam. *Harry Houdini.* Lucent, 1995.

For Older Readers (ages 15 and up)

Allen, Woody. *Play It Again, Sam.* Random House, 1969.

Allen, Woody. *Without Feathers.* Ballantine, 1986.

Bar-Lev, Geoffrey and Joyce Sakkal. *Jewish American Struggle for Equality.* Rourke, 1992.

Benny, Jack. *Sunday Nights at Seven: The Jack Benny Story.* Warner, 1990.

Bergreen, Laurence. *As Thousands Cheer: The Life of Irving Berlin.* Da Capo, 1996.

Bernstein, Leonard. *Leonard Bernstein's Young People's Concerts.* Doubleday, 1992.

Blume, Judy. *Tiger Eyes.* Simon & Schuster, 1982.

Brownstone, David M. *Jewish American Heritage.* Facts on File, 1988.

Dershowitz, Alan. *Chutzpah.* Simon & Schuster, 1992.

Ferber, Elizabeth. *Pop Culture Legends: Groucho Marx.* Chelsea House, 1995.

Ferber, Elizabeth. *Pop Culture Legends: Steven Spielberg.* Chelsea House, 1996.

Freedman, Suzanne. *Louis Brandeis: The People's Justice.* Enslow Pub., 1996.

Friedan, Betty. *The Feminine Mystique: Twentieth Anniversary Edition.* Norton, 1983.

Gates, Fay C. *Judaism.* Facts on File, 1991.

Gay, Kathyln and Martin. *Emma Goldman.* Lucent Bks., 1996.

Glade, Mary E. and James R. Giese. *Immigration: Diversity & National Identity.* Social Science Ed., 1988.

Greenberg, Judith E. *Newcomers to America: Stories of Today's Young Immigrants.* Franklin Watts, 1996.

Handler, Andrew and Susan V. Meschel. *Young People Speak: Surviving the Holocaust in Hungary.* Franklin Watts, 1993.

Harris, Bertha. *Gertrude Stein.* Chelsea House, 1995.

Hoff, Mark. *Gloria Steinem: The Women's Movement.* Millbrook Press, 1991.

Lacey, Robert. *Little Man: Meyer Lansky & the Gangster Life.* Little Brown, 1991.

Landau, Elaine. *We Survived the Holocaust.* Franklin Watts, 1991.

Lanes, Selma G. *The Art of Maurice Sendak.* Abrams, 1984.

Langer, Lawrence. *Holocaust Testimonies: The Ruins of Memory.* Yale Univ. Press, 1991.

Lazo, Caroline. *Elie Wiesel.* Silver Burdett, 1994.

Leinwand, Gerald. *American Immigration: Should the Open Door Be Closed?* Franklin Watts, 1995.

Lord, James. *Six Exceptional Women.* Farrar Straus Giroux, 1994.

Lowe, Sue Davidson. *Stieglitz: A Memoir-Biography.* Farrar Straus Giroux, 1983.

Meachum, Virginia. *Steven Spielberg: Hollywood Filmmaker.* Enslow, 1996.

Miller, Arthur. *Arthur Miller in Conversation.* Contemp. Res., 1993.

Miller, Arthur. *The Crucible.* Viking Penguin, 1995.

Pascoe, Elaine. *Racial Prejudice: Why Can't We Overcome?* Franklin Watts, 1997.

Patterson, Charles. *Anti-Semitism: The Road to the Holocaust & Beyond.* Walker, 1989.

Richardson, Susan. *Pop Culture Legends: Bob Dylan.* Chelsea House, 1995.

Riese, Randall. *Her Name Is Barbra: An Intimate Portrait of the Real Barbra Streisand.* Carol Pub. Group, 1993.

Russell, Charles E. *Haym Salomon & the Revolution.* Rprt. Serv., 1993.

Segal, Sheila F. *Women of Valor: Stories of Great Jewish Women Who Helped Shape the Twentieth Century.* Behrman, 1996.

Seinfeld, Jerry. *SeinLanguage.* Bantam, 1993.

Spada, James. *Streisand: Her Life.* Random House, 1995.

Steinem, Gloria. *Moving Beyond Words.* Simon & Schuster, 1994.

Strahinich, Helen. *Holocaust: Understanding & Remembering.* Enslow, 1996.

Tomlinson, Michael. *Jonas Salk.* Rourke, 1993.

Van Steenwyk, Elizabeth. *Levi Strauss: The Blue Jeans Man.* Walker, 1988.

Westerfeld, Scott. *Watergate.* Silver Burdett, 1991.

Wiesel, Elie. *All Rivers Run to the Sea: Memoirs.* Knopf, 1995.

Wiesel, Elie. *Night.* Bantam, 1982.

ONLINE SITES AND ORGANIZATIONS

Alan Dershowitz
http://counterpoint.mit.edu/v10/n5/dersh.html
Lengthy interview with the nation's most prominent defense attorney, in which he discusses (among other topics) his Jewish heritage.

American Jewish Committee
165 East 56th Street
New York, NY 10022
http://www.ajc.org:80/
Organization whose mission is to assure the creative survival of Jews in the United States and abroad, and support for Israel's peace and security.

American Jewish Historical Society
2 Thornton Road
Waltham, MA 02154
http://www.ajhs.org/index.htm
Located on the campus of Brandeis University, this organization collects published material and artwork on the history of the American Jewish community.

American Society for Jewish Music
170 West 74th Street
New York, NY 10023
Informs the general music public about the wide and rich dimensions of Jewish music.

Anti-Defamation League
823 UN Plaza
New York, NY 10017-3560
http://www.adl.org/
The home page of the world's leading organization that fights anti-Semitism.

The Ayn Rand Institue
http://www.aynrand.org/entry.html
Writings by and about author **Ayn Rand,** whose philosophy, Objectivism, continues to influence people more than a decade after her death.

Barbara Boxer
http://www.senate.gov/member/ca/boxer/general/
The California senator's home page on the U.S. Senate website.

Barry Levinson
http://www.levinson.com/
Official website for the director of such films as *Rain Man, Sleepers, Avalon,* and the producer of the television shows *Homicide* and *Oz.*

The Basketball Hall of Fame
P.O. Box 179
1150 West Columbus Ave.
Springfield, MA 01101-0179
http://www.hoophall.com/
Where hoops legends **Red Auerbach, Dolph Schayes,** and **Nat Holman** are enshrined.

Ben & Jerry's Ice Cream
http://www.benjerry.com
Home page of the fabulous flavor duo Ben & Jerry (**Ben Cohen** and **Jerry Greenfield).** A fun-filled activity page for kids and adults features contests, puzzles, a new-flavor list (including Kosher flavors!).

Bernstein Studio

http://www.leonardbernstein.com/studio/

The official site dedicated to preserving **Leonard Bernstein's** legacy features numerous newspaper articles by and about Bernstein, photos from his long career, and audio clips of him speaking and performing.

B'nai B'rith

http://bnaibrith.org/

Official website for one of the world's leading Jewish charitable organizations.

Bob Dylan Homepage

http://www.bobdylan.com/

Official site for Dylan fans, including news about the rock 'n' roll legend's concerts and new releases, and audio clips of his music.

Bob Dylan: Tangled Up in Jews

http://www.well.com/user/yudel/dylan.html

For those already educated in folk music, Jewish music, and Dylan, this site provides a close look at the Jewish influences in the music and lyrics of Bob Dylan. (The site's title is a pun on Dylan's song "Tangled Up in Blue.")

Boston Celtics

http://www.nba.com/celtics/00400470.html

Read all about the history of the greatest franchise in basketball history and how **Red Auerbach** made the Celtics into champions.

Brandeis-Bardin Institute

1101 Peppertree Lane
Brandeis, CA 93064

Institute founded by **Louis Brandeis** features a youth campus whose task is to discover various methods and approaches to making Judaism meaningful in individuals' lives.

Brandeis University

http://www.brandeis.edu/overview/historical.html

Website for the university named for Supreme Court Justice **Louis Brandeis** includes a history of the university.

Carl Sagan Tribute Site

http://wwwvms.utexas.edu/~mrapp/sagan/sagan.html

Honoring one of the great scientists of the 20th century (a site heavy with graphics—for fast computers only).

Council for Jewish Education

426 W. 58th Street
New York, NY 10019

Organization whose mission is to further the cause of Jewish education in America.

Diane Feinstein

http://www.senate.gov/~feinstein/index.html

The California senator's home page on the U.S. Senate's website.

Dreamworks SKG

http://www.ibm.com/thinkmag/features/katz2.html

Home page of the entertainment company founded by Jewish Americans **Steven Spielberg, David Geffen,** and **Jeffrey Katzenberg.** See sneak previews of movies-in-the-making.

Dustin Hoffman

http://www.celebsite.com/people/dustinhoffman/index.html

Biography, photos, filmography, and links on the actor who has played everyone from Tootsie to Rain Man to the Marathon Man.

Ellis Island

http://www.ellisisland.org/

Explore Ellis Island and its fascinating immigration museum online.

The Forward

http://www.forward.com/

Online home for the New York newspaper that has for a century published news about Jewish issues in America and abroad. The *Forward's* online archives provide a wealth of information about the Jewish-American experience.

George Gershwin

http://www.classical.net/~music/comp.lst/gershwin.html

Biography, discography, and numerous links about America's most famous composer.

George Steinbrenner

http://www.yankees.com/web/home/main.html

Information about the controversial baseball owner on the New York Yankees website.

Helen Frankenthaler

http://www.nmwa.org/legacy/bios/bfranken.htm

Biography of the artist (with links to online images of her art) posted by the National Museum of Women in the Arts.

Holocaust Survivors Memorial Foundation

800 5th Avenue
New York, NY 10021

Teaches Americans about the history and current implications of the Holocaust. Conducts research and conferences, maintains Holocaust materials, and supports projects in areas such as motion pictures, books, opera, and television programs

Houdini Historical Center
330 E. College Avenue
Appleton, WI 54911
Organization interested in preserving the life and achievements of magician **Harry Houdini.**

Isaac Bashevis Singer
http://nobelprizes.com/nobel/literature/1978a.html
A page of links regarding the Nobel Prize–winning author.

Jerry Seinfeld
http://www.celebsite.com/people/jerryseinfeld/index.html
Provides fans with a personal biography, vital statistics, reviews, and other websites on one of America's most popular comedians.

Jewhoo!
http://www.jewhoo.com/
Humorous parody of the search engine *Yahoo!* that provides links for dozens of famous people are Jewish.

Jewish American Hall of Fame
http://www.amuseum.org/jahf/
Honoring achievers in the arts, business, and politics; includes almost all of the people (and more!) described in this book.

Jewish Defense Organization Youth Movement
134 W. 32nd Street, Room 602
New York, NY 10001
Jewish youths unite together to voice their concerns about anti-Semitism.

Jewish Family and Life
http://www.jewishfamily.com/
Webzine featuring articles about the modern Jewish family.

JewishGen
http://www.jewishgen.org/
Online site provides search databases for individuals to trace the genealogy of their Jewish roots.

The Jewish Museum of New York
1109 Fifth Avenue
New York, NY 10128
http://www.Jewishmuseum.org/
Highlights four thousand years of Jewish history through exhibits, films, lectures, and concerts.

Jewish War Veterans of the U.S.A.
1811 R Street, NW
Washington, DC 20009
Maintains National Service Offices throughout the country and provides a voice on Capitol Hill for veterans' legislation and issues of concern to the Jewish community.

Jewish Women International
1828 L Street, NW
Suite 250
Washington, DC 20036
Engages in activities that support women and their families. Founded and maintains a residential treatment center for emotionally disturbed children in Jerusalem.

The Jolson Society
http://www.btinternet.com/~jolson/main.htm
Website devoted to exploring the phenomenon of **Al Jolson's** enduring fame.

Jonas Salk
http://www.teenaids-peercorps.com/2eJonasSalk.html
Interview with **Jonas Salk** by TeenAIDS, an Internet AIDS-awareness group, in which Salk compares his work in polio research to today's AIDS crisis.

Jonas Salk Obituary
http://www.sddt.com/files/library/95headlines/DN95_06_26/STORY95_06_26_02.html
A lengthy obituary of **Jonas Salk** published in upon his death in June 1995 in the San Diego *Source.*

Levi Strauss Company
http://www.levistrauss.com
Website for the clothing company offering product information and historical information about **Levi Strauss.**

Madeleine K. Albright
http://secretary.state.gov/
The secretary of state's home page on the U.S. State Department's website.

Man Ray
http://www.manraytrust.com/
Official site for viewing the photographs of the visionary artist, **Man Ray.**

National Center for Jewish Film
Brandeis University
Lown Building, Room 102
Waltham, MA 02254-9110
Provides film material relevant to the Jewish experience.

National Jewish Committee on Scouting
c/o Boy Scouts of America
1325 W. Walnut Hill Lane
P.O. Box 152079
Irving, TX 75015-2079
Assists national and local Jewish organizations interested in promoting and strengthening Jewish identities through scouting programs.

National Jewish Girl Scout Committee
33 Central Drive
Bronxville, NY 10708
Promotes and encourages girl scouting within the Jewish community and related award programs and religious services.

National Museum of American Jewish Military History
1811 R Street, NW
Washington, DC 20009
Multinational organization dedicated to preserving the memorabilia of Jews who served in the U.S. armed forces, and to educating the public about their contributions to America's freedom.

The Pulitzer Prize
http://www.pulitzer.org/navigation/index.html
Official website for the most prestigious American awards in literature, drama, and music, founded by **Joseph Pulitzer.**

Remember: Cybrary of the Holocaust
http://remember.org/
An exhaustive online resource providing text and images on the Holocaust, including segments designed for students.

Sammy Davis, Jr.
http://www.interlog.com/~wad/sambio.html
Lengthy biography of the legendary entertainer, including information on his conversion to Judaism.

SICSA—The Vidal Sassoon International Center for the Study of Anti-Semitism
The Hebrew University of Jerusalem
Mount Scopus
91905 Jerusalem
Israel
http://www2.huji.ac.il/www_jcd/top.html
A website dedicated to the research of anti-Semitism, focusing on relations between Jews and non-Jews.

Simon Wiesenthal Center

http://www.wiesenthal.com/

Home page for one of the world's leading centers on Holocaust education.

Sparks

http://www.sparksmag.com/

An online magazine for kids about all things Jewish: celebrities, issues, anti-Semitism, and fiction.

Statue of Liberty–Ellis Island Foundation

52 Vanderbilt Avenue
New York, NY 10017

Organization devoted to the restoration of Ellis Island and the Statue of Liberty in an effort to foster and promote public knowledge of and interest in the history of both monuments.

Stephen Sondheim Stage

http://www.sondheim.com/news.html

Official site for news about America's most prolific and respected living stage composer.

Supreme Court Biographies

http://www.courttv.com/library/supreme/justices/

Biographies of the current U.S. Supreme Court justices (including **Ruth Bader Ginsberg** and **Stephen Breyer**) on a site maintained by Court TV.

Survivors of the Shoah Foundation

http://www.vhf.org/

Founded by **Steven Spielberg** in 1994, this nonprofit organization is dedicated to video-taping and archiving interviews of Holocaust survivors all over the world.

United Jewish Appeal–Federation of Jewish Philanthropies of New York

130 E. 59th Street
New York, NY 10022

Agencies that provide hospital, health, family and child care services, and Jewish education to individuals in the greater New York area, Israel, and thirty-four other countries.

United States Holocaust Memorial Museum

100 Raoul Wallenberg Place, SW
Washington, DC 20024-2150
http:www.ushmm.org/index.html

Museum that preserves the memory of the millions of people murdered in the Holocaust.

Virtual Jerusalem

www.virtual.co.il/

Site organized by neighborhoods that focus on different aspects of Jewish religion, culture, and communal life.

Woody Allen
http://www.celebsite.com/people/woodyallen/index.html
Website highlights the life and works of **Woody Allen.**

World Council of Jewish Archives
American Jewish Historical Society
Brandeis University
2 Thornton Road
Waltham, MA 02154
Archives and research libraries containing records of Jewish individuals, institutions, and organizations.

Films and Videos

As explored in the chapter beginning on page 91 of this book, Jewish producers, directors, writers, and actors have driven the Hollywood entertainment industry from its beginnings in the early 20th century. It is interesting to note, however, that although American Jews provided the creative force behind vast numbers of Hollywood movies, relatively few movies before the 1960s dealt directly with Jewish issues or Jewish characters. Then, Jewish-themed entertainment began coming out of Hollywood in droves. Many Jewish celebrities, such as Barbra Streisand and Woody Allen, rose to national stardom by *emphasizing* their Jewish "traits" and heritage, rather than by blending in with the the non-Jewish majority. Thus the 1960s and 1970s were somewhat of a "golden age" of Jews in Hollywood. Since then, however, the intensity and quantity of Jewish-themed movies has decreased.

Listed below is a selective collection of American movies that serves as an interesting portrait of how Jews have been depicted in Hollywood entertainment for the last half-century. All are readily available on videotape.

NOTE: Movies are grouped by appropriateness for age groups; in all cases, however, parental guidance and permission is recommended.

For Viewers Up to Age 12 (rated G and PG)

The Chosen (1981)
Directed by: Jeremy Paul Kagan
Starring: Maximilian Schell, Rod Steiger, Robby Benson
Set in 1940s New York, a story of an unlikely friendship between two teenage boys—one from a strict, Orthodox family, the other from a more assimilated, Conservative background.

Crossfire (1947)
Directed by: Edward Dmytryk
Starring: Robert Young, Robert Mitchum, Robert Ryan, Gloria Grahame
A military murder mystery that was one of the first mainstream Hollywood movies to deal openly with anti-Semitism.

The Diary of Anne Frank (1959)
Directed by: George Stevens
Starring: Millie Perkins, Shelley Winters, Richard Beymer, Lou Jacobi, Ed Wynn
Film version of the stage play based on the diary entries written by a teenage girl hiding from the Nazis for more than two years in an office building attic.

Duck Soup (1933)
Directed by: Leo McCarey
Starring: The Marx Brothers
This film is considered by many to be the greatest of the films starring **Groucho Marx** and his hilarious brothers (but a viewing of *The Cocoanuts, Animal Crackers, Horse Feathers,* or *A Night at the Opera* will provide an equally good view of what made the Marx Brothers great).

Exodus (1960)
Directed by: Otto Preminger
Starring: Paul Newman, Eva Marie Saint
The founding of the state of Israel, told in epic, Hollywood style.

Fiddler on the Roof (1971)
Directed by: Norman Jewison
Starring: Topol, Norma Crane, Leonard Frey, Molly Picon
Film adaptation of what was once the longest-running show in Broadway history. The story, based on those of famed Yiddish writer Sholom Aleichem, tells of Tevye the Milkman and how his faith in God is tested by the modern era, modern beliefs, and anti-Semitism. The soundtrack features violin solos by **Isaac Stern.**

The Frisco Kid (1979)
Directed by: Robert Aldrich
Starring: Gene Wilder, Harrison Ford
The adventures of an immigrant Polish rabbi as he ventures across the Old West to establish a congregation in San Francisco.

Funny Girl (1968)
Directed by: William Wyler
Starring: Barbra Streisand, Omar Sharif
Barbra Streisand's triumphant, Oscar-winning screen debut is the film biography of vaudeville star Fanny Brice.

The Jazz Singer (1933)
Directed by: Alan Crosland
Starring: Al Jolson
The first feature-length movie to include sound, this historic film made **Al Jolson** into a worldwide star.

For Viewers Age 13 to 15 (rated PG-13)

Annie Hall (1977)
Directed by: Woody Allen
Starring: Woody Allen, Diane Keaton, Tony Roberts
The most successful movie of **Woody Allen's** career. The romantic comedy focuses on the love affair between a Jew (Allen) and a non-Jew (Keaton) and the hilarious interaction between their cultures.

Avalon (1990)
Directed by: Barry Levinson
Starring: Armin Mueller-Stahl, Elizabeth Perkins, Joan Plowright, Kevin Pollak, Aidan Quinn, Elijah Wood
Touching story of how an immigrant Jewish family came to Baltimore at the turn of the century and then gradually splintered apart as generations passed.

Brighton Beach Memoirs (1986)
Directed by: Gene Saks
Starring: Jonathan Silverman
Autobiographical movie by writer Neil Simon about his youth in Brooklyn and his entry into the world of comedy writing.

Driving Miss Daisy (1989)
Directed by: Bruce Beresford
Starring: Morgan Freeman, Jessica Tandy, Dan Aykroyd
Story of an elderly, Jewish Southern widow who must adjust her attitudes about race and prejudice to accept the assistance and friendship of an African-American chauffeur hired by her son.

Gentleman's Agreement (1947)
Directed by: Elia Kazan
Starring: Gregory Peck, Dorothy McGuire, John Garfield
The film that brought anti-Semitism out of hiding in Hollywood. Gregory Peck stars as a non-Jewish journalist who poses as a Jew to research anti-Semitism in America. He finds that just by using a "Jewish name" (Green), he is treated as a second-class citizen in many ways.

Holocaust (1978, television mini-series)
Directed by: Marvin J. Chomsky
Starring: Meryl Streep, James Woods, Ian Holm
Groundbreaking television movie that tells the stories of each member of a German Jewish family attempting to survive the Nazi Holocaust.

Lies My Father Told Me (1975)
Directed by: Ján Kadár
Starring: Yossi Yadin, Jeffrey Lynas
Canadian film about young boy whose parents want him to assimilate and who disapprove of his affection for his Old World Jewish grandfather.

The Pawnbroker (1965)
Directed by: Sidney Lumet
Starring: Rod Steiger
One of the first films to deal with the effects of the Holocaust on its survivors living in the United States. Tells the story of the tortured life of concentration camp survivor Sol Nazerman, operator of a pawn shop in the heart of Harlem in New York City.

Quiz Show (1994)
Directed by: Robert Redford
Starring: Ralph Fiennes, John Turturro, Rob Morrow
Based on the true story of a scandal over television game show contestants being fed answers to the on-air quizzes. The film also exlpores how anti-Semitism was an everpresent undercurrent in 1950s America.

School Ties (1992)
Directed by: Robert Mandel
Starring: Brendan Fraser, Matt Damon, Chris O'Donnell
Story of a working-class Jewish athlete who wins a football scholarship to Gentile prep school and is instructed to keep his religion a secret from his classmates.

The Sunshine Boys (1975)
Directed by: Herbert Ross
Starring: Walter Matthau, George Burns
Adapted by **Neil Simon** from his stage play, this film affectionately tells the story of a vaudeville comedy team who can't stop fighting when they try to reunite in old age.

West Side Story (1961)
Directed by Jerome Robbins, Robert Wise
Starring: Natalie Wood, Richard Beymer, Rita Moreno
Considered one of the finest musicals, this is the film version of the stage show featuring the music of **Leonard Bernstein** and the lyrics of **Stephen Sondheim**.

Yentl (1983)
Directed by: Barbra Streisand
Starring: Barbra Streisand, Amy Irving, Mandy Patinkin
Adapted from a story by Yiddish author **Isaac Bashevis Singer,** many people believe this to be **Barbra Streisand's** best filmmaking achievement. The film tells the story of an Orthodox girl who so much wants to study the Torah that she poses as a boy to partake in male-only classes.

For Viewers 16 and Older (rated R)

Crimes and Misdemeanors (1989)
Directed by: Woody Allen
Martin Landau, Anjelica Huston, Woody Allen, Alan Alda, Sam Waterston
Perhaps **Woody Allen's** most serious film about religion and morality.

The Producers (1968)
Directed by: Mel Brooks
Starring: Zero Mostel, Gene Wilder
A landmark film in that it brought the most audacious, sarcastic, and sacriligious aspects of Jewish humor to the big screen and won widespread audience appeal.

Schindler's List (1993)
Directed by: Steven Spielberg
Starring: Liam Neeson, Ben Kingsley, Ralph Fiennes
Deemed one of the most important films of all time, **Steven Spielberg's** masterpiece explores the Holocaust in a realistic, intense, and very disturbing manner. The story concerns Oskar Schindler, a non-Jewish businessman who seeks to make a fortune during the Holocaust by using concentration camp prisoners as cheap labor in his factory. In the process, his eyes are open to the evil of the Nazi regime, and Schindler shifts his motive from profit-making to saving lives. The film swept the Academy Awards and revitalized interest in preserving the memory of the Holocaust.

Shoah (1985)
Directed by: Claude Lanzmann
Not easy or entertaining in any way, this 9 1/2-hour documentary is the definitive film history of the Holocaust. Without using any archival footage, filmmaker Lanzmann tells the story completely through modern interviews with Holocaust survivors, witnesses, and ex-Nazis.

Index